LEADER'S GUIDE

Focus on the Family® Presents

DR. JAMES DOBSON'S
bringing up boys™

video seminar
12 sessions for groups

LEADER'S GUIDE

Focus on the Family® Presents

DR. JAMES DOBSON'S
bringing up boys™

To order additional copies of the Participant's Guide, please call Focus on the Family at 1-800-A-Family or order online at www.family.org. This book is also available at your local Christian bookstore.

Printed in the United States of America

03 04 05 06 07 08 / 10 9 8 7 6 5 4 3 2

ISBN 1-58997-101-9

TABLE OF CONTENTS

INTRODUCTION:
how to use this guide

Welcome to the Leader's Guide for the *Bringing Up Boys*™ video series featuring Dr. James Dobson. This book has one aim: to help you lead successful group discussions of the series' video segments.

And what is a successful group discussion?

It's lively. In each session plan you'll find plenty of provocative questions that get people talking and thinking. Use those queries to break the ice at the start of each meeting, and to help group members zero in on key points from Dr. Dobson's informative, often humorous presentations.

It's life related. Each session is designed to help participants connect the principles of *Bringing Up Boys*™ to their unique families. In-the-group and at-home activities keep things down-to-earth and practical.

It's life changing. Every session plan spells out its goal of altering attitudes and equipping group members to take specific action. That's why each meeting includes Bible study for the heart, information for the head, and activities for the home.

In addition to the videos and this Leader's Guide, you'll need a Participant's Guide for each group member. That's the "student book" that helps each person prepare for the meeting, take notes on the video, and work through exercises that apply the principles to everyday life.

FAQ'S: FEARFULLY ASKED QUESTIONS

Q: How should we use the Participant's Guide?

A: Make sure each person has one. Encourage people to read and respond to the "Quotes and Questions" section before each meeting. Have group members take notes during the video in the "Video Journal" section. You'll use the "Scriptures to Study" and "Apply It" sections during your meeting, assuming you have time. "Try It" should be saved for people to use during the week.

Q: Is there a video for each session?

A: Yes—except for Session 12. That's a review, discussing and applying the principles of the previous sessions.

Q: Our meetings aren't very long. How can we cover all the material?

A: If you're on a tight schedule, some video segments may not leave you a great deal of discussion time. Here are two ways to adapt the material for shorter sessions:

Option 1:

Condense the session plan. Skip Step 1, "Welcome the Group." Go directly to Step 2, "Watch the Video." Then, rather than using the discussion questions in Step 3, "Wrestle with the Principles," simply ask, "What principle from this video would you most like to apply this week, and why?" Close by reading the Scriptures listed, and encourage people to meditate on them during the week. Have group members use both the "Apply It" and "Try It" sections of the Participant's Guide at home.

Option 2:

Extend the length of the course. For example, you might take two meetings to cover a session. During the first meeting, watch the video segment and let people react to it. During the second meeting, summarize the video segment and continue the discussion, using Step 3 of the session plan. After working through the "Apply It" section of the Participant's Guide, take time for people to plan how they'll use the "Try It" exercises and to pray for each other.

Q: How much time do I have to spend preparing for each session?

A: As much or as little as you like. We'd recommend watching the video segment before the meeting if you can, but it's not absolutely necessary. Reading the session plan, including the brief Bible passages listed, will make you a more confident leader—and will allow you to decide in advance where you might need to skip sections in the interest of time. Gathering materials can be done quickly; all you'll need, in addition to the video and equipment to show it, are pens or pencils and extra copies of the Participant's Guide for visitors.

Q: *Our group includes parents, grandparents, parents-to-be, and people who are just interested in the subject of raising boys. How can I make this apply to all of them?*

A: Acknowledge the variety in your group at the beginning of the course. Instead of always referring to "your sons," you might sometimes use phrases like, "the boys in your life," "the boys you love," and "the boys you may care for someday." When questions or exercises in the course ask group members to think about a specific boy, encourage those who don't have sons to think about a grandson, nephew, neighbor, or student.

Q. *The single moms in our group face a special challenge in raising boys. How can I make sure their concerns are addressed?*

A. Wherever possible, activities and questions have been designed to apply both to single parents and couples. So that single parents don't feel left out, avoid breaking the group into married couples for working through the "Apply It" activities or for prayer times; try forming groups of three to five instead. Dr. Dobson deals in this series with the need for single moms to find male role models for their sons. He offers additional advice for single mothers in his book, *Bringing Up Boys*™ (Tyndale House).

Q: *What if group members disagree with each other, or with Dr. Dobson? How can I handle that?*

A: Relax. Your job is getting people to think through what it means to raise healthy boys—not getting them to agree with the featured speaker or with each other. Resist the temptation to provide the "right" answer to every question; affirm as many opinions as you can. Invite open, honest discussion; if one or two group members dominate or disrupt, solicit responses from others. When there's disagreement, encourage people to find and study related Bible passages and to come to their own conclusions.

Q: *What if I ask a question and nobody has an answer? How can I keep the discussion going?*

A: Don't panic. Silence can be a good thing. It may even mean people are thinking. If you sense group members don't want to answer a question because it's too personal, just encourage them to think about their responses. Be prepared with a few examples from your own life to prime the pump. Sometimes rephrasing a question helps. When people are intimidated by the size of the group or the dominance of a few outspoken participants, let them turn to a neighbor and answer a question. And be sure to react as positively as you can when you do get a response; people won't want to participate if they think their answers will be ignored or rejected.

Q: *How can I tell which parts of the session plan to say word for word, which parts to summarize in my own words, and which parts are answers to questions?*

A: Things you might say word-for-word to the group are in bold type; information you might paraphrase is in regular type; answers are in parentheses. But we encourage you to use your own words anytime! And keep in mind that the answers are *suggestions*, included for your benefit in case the group seems stumped. Your participants' answers can—and should—vary.

BOYS WILL BE BOYS

PURPOSE: To help participants appreciate the unique characteristics of boys, and to suggest some ways in which they can celebrate "Male Appreciation Week" at home.

PASSAGES: Genesis 1:27; 1 Kings 2:1–4; Job 38:3

PREPARATION:
- If possible, watch video 1 in advance. Approximate running time: 60 minutes. If you expect your meeting time to be short, see the Introduction to this guide for ideas on adapting the session plan.

- Make sure each person has a copy of the Participant's Guide; you may want to bring extras for visitors.

- Provide pens or pencils.

- Set up a television and video player in your meeting place.

PREVIEW: Here's a summary of the principles in video 1:

Boys are definitely different from girls. Despite this common-sense observation, the "unisex" concept took hold in the early 1970s. According to this view, males and females are identical except in the ability to bear children. Parents were told that boys and girls should be raised identically—and especially that boys should be taught to be more like girls.

The unisex hypothesis was destroyed when scientists, using newly developed imaging techniques, saw differences in male and female brain structure. And as the influence of hormones on brain development and behavior were better understood, it became clear that the differences between boys and girls weren't just cultural. Boys are naturally more aggressive, take more risks, talk less, are more competitive, and find it harder to sit still.

So is masculinity bad, something to be "fixed"? Some would have us believe that, but God designed boys as they are because He wanted them that way—to grow up to be protectors and providers. The boyish traits that can irritate parents should be enjoyed and celebrated—as well as molded and civilized. That's how to prepare boys for manhood.

STEP
1

WELCOME
the group

Say something like this:

Welcome to the first session in Dr. James Dobson's video series based on his book *Bringing Up Boys*.

Introduce yourself. If your group isn't too large, let people introduce themselves, too, and give them the option of telling something they hope to gain from these sessions. Then ease into the topic with a few questions like the following.

How many here are parents of boys? As needed, affirm parents, grandparents, those who are attending because they're raising someone else's boys—and those who simply care about boys in general.

How many would agree that boys are more difficult to raise than girls?

There's no need to reach a consensus on this question. Let a few volunteers give reasons for their answers.

If you could ask a psychologist one question about boys, what would it be?

After listening to a few replies, note that you have such a person with you—on video. Explain that Dr. James Dobson is founder and president of Focus on the Family. A licensed psychologist, he holds a Ph.D. in child development—and with his wife Shirley has raised a son as well as a daughter.

Then say something like this: **People may disagree about whether it's tougher to raise boys or girls. Either way, raising healthy boys isn't easy, especially today. In these videos, Dr. Dobson helps us understand why boys are the way they are— and what we can do to meet their special needs. In the first segment, we'll look at "typical boy" behaviors that sometimes threaten to drive us crazy.**

WATCH
the video

With the group, watch video segment 1, "Boys Will Be Boys." Encourage participants to take notes in the "Video Journal" section of the Participant's Guide. Pass out pens or pencils as needed.

WRESTLE
with the principles

Discuss the video, using questions and comments along the following lines.

What are some "typical boy" behaviors? Opinions will vary, but boys generally tend to be dominant, competitive, rule makers, explorers, hunters, builders, destroyers, and weapon makers. They're prone to seek power, fame, glory, fights, and risks, and they tend to prefer action over thinking and feeling.

Which of the "typical boy" behaviors mentioned in the video describe the boys you know best?

Which of those behaviors challenge you the most?

Did the video change the way you see those behaviors, or the way you see your responses to them? If so, how?

Call the group's attention to Genesis 1:27, I Kings 2:1–4, and Job 38:3 in the "Scriptures to Study" section of the Participant's Guide. Discuss the passages, using questions and comments like the following.

Genesis 1:27
Some have suggested that "male" and "female" are just cultural concepts, and that a "unisex" approach should be taken to child rearing. How does this verse shed light on that issue? (God created two distinct genders, a difference that transcends culture and time. We ignore that difference at our own risk.)

I Kings 2:1–4; Job 38:3
What do these verses imply about the differences between males and females? (That there is such a thing as distinctly masculine behavior. In these cases, masculinity is associated with strength, an ability to stand firm in a stressful situation.)

Which masculine characteristics do you believe are God given, and which might be learned or based on individual temperament? Opinions may vary widely; don't worry if there's strong disagreement. Dr. Dobson will have more to say about masculine traits in future video segments. Point out that your focus in this course isn't simply to talk about "typical" boys but to recognize the unique traits and special needs of the specific boys for whom group members are responsible.

After wrapping up the Scripture discussion, direct the group to the "Apply It" section of the Participant's Guide. Thumbnail versions of these pages are at the end of the session. Depending on the size and makeup of your group, people can work on this as individuals, pairs, teams based on the ages of participants' boys, or teams based simply on personal interest.

Allow a few minutes for this activity; then regather the group. Discuss results, using questions and comments like the following.

Preschool:
As needed, note that the more Susan understands her son's behavior, the better she'll be able to cope with it. His activity level isn't unusual for boys of that age, and knowing that may keep her expectations realistic. Talking to parents of other boys Peter's age might help Susan to know she's not alone. If Peter is defiant—that is, if Susan warns him not to drop a toy on the floor, and he does it anyway—she can levy an appropriate penalty.

Elementary:
As people share results, encourage them to explain why they designed the theme park as they did. Do any patterns emerge? Do the boys represented by your group tend to be risk takers with high energy levels? Are they especially interested in building, science, or math? Urge participants to give more thought this week to the question of whether their home environments could be rearranged to better accommodate the needs of their boys.

Adolescence:
Answers may vary widely, as parents see differently the safety of various activities. Rather than letting the discussion turn into a debate on the merits of bungee jumping or target shooting, ask people to share the reasons behind their replies. If group members express concern about some of the pastimes their teen boys are involved in, you may want to remember this later when you close the session in prayer.

S T E P

WRAP UP
the session

Explain that in the next session, you'll discuss how to help boys deal with some of the forces that tend to get them into trouble.

Pray for group members, thanking God for the care and concern they show for boys. Ask God to guide people in applying what they learned; if appropriate, include specific concerns that arose in discussion.

Call attention to the "Try It" section of the Participant's Guide. Encourage group members to consider the suggestions for creating "Male Appreciation Week" at home.

DR. JAMES DOBSON'S bringing up boys

Apply It: *Preschool:*

Susan is at her wit's end with four-year-old Peter. He's always getting into things. His favorite game is to play racetrack with toy cars—which inevitably ends with a vehicle crashing through Lego barriers and sending pieces flying everywhere.

Nothing in the house that has a handle, lever, or tail has escaped his curiosity. He especially likes things that make a lot of noise—like piano keys and dropping dump trucks on tile floors. He wonders why Mom isn't more grateful for the knowledge he's given her: She knows exactly how many shoes the laundry hamper will hold, how to get Play-Doh out of a drain, and how much toothpaste a cat can eat before throwing up on the bed.

How might Susan's stress level be reduced by understanding what's "normal" for a boy like Peter?

What steps could Susan take to maintain her sanity while letting her "boy be a boy"?

12

---

session 1: BOYS WILL BE BOYS

Elementary:

Pretend you're going to design a theme park for a boy you're raising, or another boy you know well.

What would the theme be?

What kind of rides would it have? (For example, if the boy is a thrill-seeker, he might like a loop-the-loop roller coaster; if he's into science, he might prefer a space shuttle that makes him weightless.)

Could any aspects of this theme park be worked into your son's real world? How? (For instance, does he need more room to run? Would he like to redecorate his room to reflect an interest in tigers? Could you and he make an "asteroid cruiser" out of cardboard boxes, or a wagon with streamers?)

13

Adolescence:

Consider the following "risky behaviors." Which would you allow a teenager on a "boys will be boys" basis? Which would you ban? Which would you allow under certain conditions? Why?

	"Never!"	*"Yes…Under these conditions."*
dirt biking		
skydiving		
rock climbing		
kick boxing		
bungee jumping		
party hopping		
Internet surfing		
nose piercing		
drag racing		
prank calling		
smoking		
target shooting		

Try It: *Want to show a boy that you appreciate the "boyishness" God gave him? Try celebrating "Male Appreciation Week" in your home. Here are some suggestions to get you started.*

Preschool:

Many boys love to take things apart to see how they work. If your son is like this, you've probably already encountered him "fixing" things. You can turn this into an opportunity to affirm his masculinity by finding him something interesting to "fix" together.

Maybe you have an old clock or broken household appliance that could be sacrificed. Don't worry about whether you can actually fix it (or even get all the pieces back in). The point is to encourage your son in his natural inclination.

As you dismantle the item, you might ask the boy why he enjoys this, or how he thinks the inventor invented the machine. Listen carefully to what he says and show him you're proud of him by letting him keep the finished product as his "experiment." But don't forget to tell him to ask before he tries to fix anything else!

Elementary:

Here's a "dating game"—a time for your son to "go out with" Mom. The point: to learn how a man should treat a lady.

The setting for this date might be a favorite restaurant, miniature golf course, or simply a neighbor's house. Let the boy pick the place, call to invite his date, and choose his outfit. You might even come up with a way for him to earn money to pay for the event.

Prepare the boy by telling him that he "wins the game" if his date has a nice time. You may want to give him some rules. Examples might include:

• Ladies go first when entering rooms, ordering dinner, etc.

• It's polite to open doors for her.

• When at a table or getting into a car, make sure she's seated before you are.

• When walking on the sidewalk, protect her by staying on the street side.

You might also want to practice things to say during the date—not to mention table manners.

Adolescence:

Are there any non-dangerous "risk-taking behaviors" your teen enjoys that you might be able to affirm this week?

Here are a few examples:

• Give him $10 and challenge him to invest it in some way, with the goal of doubling it in two weeks.

• If he's into public speaking, debate, or drama, congratulate him for having the courage to get up in front of people. If he's scheduled to do any of these things in a speech tournament or play, be sure to attend.

• Ask him to teach you how to use in-line skates or conquer a climbing wall.

• If he likes driving, let him chauffeur the family to a restaurant or church.

Single-Parent Tip:

If you're a single mom who doesn't feel confident about taking apart household appliances, try building something with your boy instead. It might be a puzzle, a tower of blocks, or the surface of an imaginary planet fashioned in clay.

If you're a single dad and want to try the "dating game," you may wish to enlist the help of an aunt or other relative, or a lady from church.

session **2**

THE TROUBLE WITH B⚾YS

PURPOSE:	To help group members identify and deal with the cultural and physical forces that make boys a challenge to raise.
PASSAGES:	Genesis 25:27–28; Psalm 127:3–5
PREPARATION:	• If possible, watch video 2 in advance. Approximate running time: 36 minutes. If you expect your meeting time to be short, see the Introduction to this guide for ideas on adapting the session plan.
	• Make sure each person has a copy of the Participant's Guide; you may want to bring extras for visitors.
	• Provide pens or pencils.
	• Set up a television and video player in your meeting place.

PREVIEW: Here's a summary of the principles in video 2:

Boys are in a great deal of trouble today. Recent research shows that, compared to girls, boys are more susceptible to emotional disturbances, learning problems, violent behavior, drug use, and lawbreaking.

Reasons for this vary, but at the foundation of the problem is the disintegration of the family. Many indicators, including the U.S. Census of 2001, have shown that the nuclear family is breaking down at a very rapid rate. Because of boys' volatile, unpredictable nature, this has a profound effect on their well-being.

Because boys are more unstable, more unable to cope with change, and require more structure and discipline, they need fathers to help steer them in the right direction. Because of the many factors stealing fathers away—from divorce to long hours at work—boys suffer from an absence of male role models. By providing those role models for our boys, we can begin to combat the troubles facing them.

STEP
1

WELCOME
the group

Ask: **How is it harder to raise boys today than it was when you were growing up?** (The culture is more violent; it's harder to trust people; the entertainment industry has a stronger, more negative influence; schools don't teach ethics; etc.)

How is raising boys the same as it was in the "old days"? (Boys still tend to be reckless, unruly, drawn to competition, etc.)

Ask group members to share reasons for their responses. Then say: **All of these things work together to make parenting boys a particular challenge today.**

How many of you have faced a challenge recently in raising a boy? Many will likely raise a hand.

In this video, "The Trouble With Boys," Dr. James Dobson talks about some social and physical factors faced in raising boys. He'll also focus on how to turn problems into opportunities to better understand our boys.

WATCH
the video

With the group, watch the video segment, "The Trouble With Boys." Encourage participants to take notes in the "Video Journal" section of the Participant's Guide. Pass out pens or pencils as needed.

WRESTLE
with the principles

Discuss the video, using questions and comments along the following lines.

What percentage of "boyish" behavior do you think is caused by cultural expectations? By physical and hormonal factors? Don't worry if there's disagreement; simply ask for reasons behind the answers.

Do you think "boyish" behavior is tougher on boys or on their parents?

Direct the group to the "Scriptures to Study" section of the Participant's Guide. Read Genesis 25:26–27. Then discuss the passage, using questions and comments like the following.

Why did Rebekah prefer Jacob over Esau? (Probably because she better understood Jacob, the quiet homebody.)

What did this do to the structure of the family? (It split the family into two sides.)

What advice would you give a parent who finds it hard to relate to a rambunctious boy? (One possibility: Take the time to understand and appreciate your son.)

Read the following quote from Dr. Dobson's book *Bringing Up Boys*: **"I urge you as parents not to resent or try to eliminate the aggressive and excitable nature that can be so irritating. That temperament is part of a divine plan. Celebrate it. Enjoy it. Thank God for it."**

Have a volunteer read Psalm 127:3–5. Ask: **Why do you suppose this passage singles out sons as a blessing?** As needed, point out that sons were valued for their ability to do physical work, to carry on the family line, to serve as defenders when a parent was falsely accused in court, etc. But girls are not left out (see verse 3).

Are parents in our culture likely to see sons as a blessing or not? Why?

Would you personally put sons in the "blessing" category? Explain.

Ask the group to look at the "Apply It" section of the Participant's Guide. Depending on the size and makeup of your group, have people work on this as individuals, pairs, or teams based on their boys' ages. Explain that this exercise isn't meant to indicate real hormone levels or amygdala size. It's meant as a way to show how we feel about the "normalcy" of our boys' behavior.

Allow a few minutes for the activity. Then discuss the results, using questions and comments like the following.

Where did you mark your son's testosterone level? Why?

Where did you mark your son's serotonin level? Why?

How big was the amygdala you drew? Why?

If we can't do much to change these physical factors, what can we do about "boyish" behavior that frustrates us? Note that Dr. Dobson recommends "civilizing" boys through loving discipline, and directing their energies in constructive channels. This session's "Try It" activity is designed to help with the latter.

$S^{T E}P$

4

WRAP UP
the session

In the next session, we'll look at how to protect our boys from the "Wounded Spirit" syndrome.

Pray for the group, thanking God for participants' commitment to their boys. Ask God to help people apply what they learned; as appropriate, include specific concerns that arose during the session.

Point out the "Try It" section of the Participant's Guide. Encourage people to choose and use ideas found there to steer "negative" traits in positive directions.

Apply It: Testosterone, serotonin, and the amygdala influence male behavior in ways we may never fully understand. Testosterone accounts for a boy's aggressiveness and his tendency toward dominance and competition. Low serotonin levels can make a boy more volatile and impulsive. The brain structure called the amygdala, larger in males than females, responds to perceived threats in ways that can precipitate violence.

In the first two beakers are "normal" amounts of testosterone and serotonin. The third holds a "normal"-sized amygdala. Judging from your son's usual behavior, what would you guess are his hormone levels and amygdala size? Mark your answers on the first two beakers, and draw a new amygdala in the third.

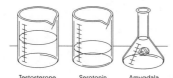

Testosterone   Serotonin   Amygdala

 Try It: *Looking to channel a boy's "problem" tendencies in a constructive direction? Try these suggestions.*

Preschool:
Risk-taking: Encourage your boy to meet a new person, try a new food, call a radio talk show (with your help), take a batch of cookies to a neighbor, or tell a friend about something he learned in church.

High energy: Have your son lead an "exercise workout" for the rest of the family, give the car or the dog a bath, or make "music" with a pots-and-pans marching band.

Elementary:
Competition: Stage contests to see who can set the table most quickly (without breaking anything), who can memorize the most Bible verses, who can give the most compliments in a day to other family members, who can stay quiet the longest, or who can rhyme the most times with "porcupine."

Boasting: Challenge your boy to create a family newsletter touting the accomplishments of everyone in your household (including pets, if you have any); to write and perform a theme song about the greatest thing he's ever done (and how he felt); or to make a collage out of magazine pictures showing "Things I'll Do When I'm 20."

Adolescence:
Love of change: Ask your son to oil a squeaky hinge, paint a dreary room, level a wobbly table, or invent a new way to recycle junk mail or pop cans; challenge him to do a service project for someone less fortunate, or write a letter to the newspaper about a problem in your town.

Curiosity about sex: Listen together to a song that mentions love or sex and talk about it; read a book by Dr. James Dobson—*Preparing for Adolescence* (Regal Books) for younger teens, or *Life on the Edge* (Word) for older ones; interview a female friend of the family about the "top ten things girls wish guys knew"; read and discuss Bible passages like Genesis 2:24, Matthew 5:28, and Psalm 119:9–11.

session **3**

WOUNDED SPIRITS

PURPOSE: To help group members prevent, identify, and counteract the "Wounded Spirit" syndrome in their boys.

PASSAGES: Psalm 102:1–11; Colossians 3:21

PREPARATION: • If possible, watch video 3 in advance. Approximate running time: 53 minutes. If you expect your meeting time to be short, see the Introduction to this guide for ideas on adapting the session plan.

• Make sure each person has a copy of the Participant's Guide; you may want to bring extras for visitors.

• Provide pens or pencils.

• Set up a television and video player in your meeting place.

PREVIEW: Here's a summary of the principles in video 3:

Many boys today have what author Frank Peretti calls "wounded spirits," a syndrome that attacks the self-image of young people. Through bullying, neglect, or abuse, many kids today become targets. The result is a crisis of confidence, self-hatred, and sometimes violent revenge.

The enormous influence of television and movies has worsened the problem by overemphasizing body image, contributing to young peoples' feelings of inadequacy. No one, including boys, is immune to it.

Boys want to be powerful and strong. When they are teased mercilessly, it can lead to the kind of rage that has surfaced in some school shootings. To prevent it, parents and other adults need to step in when boys are bullied or otherwise mistreated.

S T E P
1

WELCOME
the group

Say something like this: **Listen to the following list of characteristics. Think about which ones would concern you most if you saw them in a boy you care about.**

- **Violence**

- **Talking tough, acting rough**

- **Fear of going to school**

- **Antisocial behavior or acting "closed off"**

- **Insecurity, self-image problems**

- **Imitating peers or a lack of individuality**

Which would concern you most? Why? Let a few volunteers respond.

What might all these behaviors have in common? Explain that all are warning signs that a boy might be experiencing bullying.

Ask: **How many remember being bullied or picked on as a kid?**

That's what Dr. James Dobson will be talking about in today's video: what happens when boys are bullied, and what we can do to help them.

WATCH
the video

With the group, watch video segment 3, "Wounded Spirits." Encourage participants to take notes in the "Video Journal" section of the Participant's Guide. Pass out pens or pencils as needed.

WRESTLE
with the principles

Talk about the video, using questions and comments along the following lines.

Did this discussion of bullying bring back uncomfortable memories for anyone? Don't press for specific responses, but if people want to share, let them.

Why are those memories still powerful so many years later? (People are always vulnerable to ridicule, especially at that age, etc.)

Have group members turn to the "Scriptures to Study" section of the Participant's Guide and read Psalm 102:1–11. Then discuss the passage, using questions and comments like the following.

Which images in this passage best describe a wounded spirit to you? (Cry for help, distress, blighted heart, forgetting to eat, enemies taunt me, etc.)

What emotions did the words evoke? (Hopelessness, depression, feeling rejected, etc.)

It's not only at school that a boy's spirit can be wounded. Parents need to be on guard against wounding their children at home as well.

Read Colossians 3:21. **What are some ways in which a father might exasperate or embitter his son?** (By demanding perfection, punishing harshly, not spending time with him, etc.)

Read the following quote from Dr. Dobson's book *Bringing Up Boys:* **"One of your most important assignments as a parent is to preserve the mental and physical health of your kids. You wouldn't think of letting someone injure them physically if you could prevent it. Why, then, would you stand by and watch the spirit of your boy or girl being warped and twisted?"**

Why might a parent allow that to happen? (Might be too busy or out of touch with the child's school, or too self-absorbed to notice warning signs; might tend to minimize bullying as "part of life," etc.)

Let's look at a few ways in which we can help preserve a boy's spirit and build him up.

Direct the group to the "Apply It" section of the Participant's Guide. Thumbnail versions of these pages are at the end of the session. Depending on the size and makeup of your group, have people work on this as individuals, pairs, or teams reflecting their boys' ages.

Allow a few minutes for the activities; then regather the group. Discuss results, using questions and comments like the following.

Preschool:
1. Some possible spirit-wounding responses: "What's wrong with you?" "Don't you know better by now?" "How about being smart for a change and getting in the tub?"

Some possible spirit-preserving responses: After cooling down, say: "How'd you like a chance to break the world record for holding your breath underwater?" Or repeat your instruction firmly but calmly; administer an appropriate spank if it's not obeyed, followed by a hug.

2. Some possible spirit-wounding responses: "Quit being such a baby!" "Get over it!"

A possible spirit-preserving response: "Let's practice what you could say and do next time that happens."

Elementary:

What rules did your committee come up with? (Some possibilities: Treat others the way you want to be treated; no mean words or actions, teasing, name-calling, etc.)

How did you choose the rules?

What penalties did you want assigned? (Some possibilities: Bullies must apologize to the victim and all witnesses; parents must be held accountable, etc.)

Did you feel something like this could really work? Why or why not?

Adolescent:

Did you agree on your ratings? What might account for the differences in the way we see these events? (Painful memories from our own teen years; personality; etc.)

What does this tell you about responding to potentially spirit-wounding events in our boys' lives? As needed, point out that what may seem trivial to us might be devastating to a son, and vice versa. It's also important to understand each boy's personality and history in order to gauge the effects of bullying and embarrassment.

STEP
4

WRAP UP
the session

Explain that in the next session, you'll discuss ways to encourage healthy gender identity in boys.

Pray for group members. Ask God to guide them in applying what they learned; if appropriate, include specific concerns that arose in discussion.

Call attention to the "Try It" section of the Participant's Guide. Encourage group members to use this evaluation tool at home. If possible, refer people to your pastor or a Christian counselor if they suspect their boys are suffering from the "Wounded Spirit" syndrome.

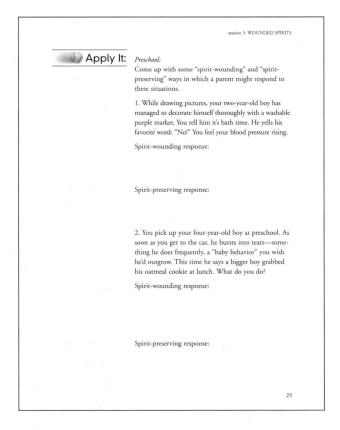

Elementary:
Pretend you're on a committee assigned to come up with a school district "anti-bullying" policy.

What rules might you include?

What would teachers and administrators need to watch for?

What penalties would you assign for infractions?

Adolescence:
Rate the following events on a scale of 1 to 10, with 10 being the most damaging, according to their ability to wound a teenage boy's spirit. If you're doing this as a team, see whether you can reach consensus on your ratings.

___ Being dumped by the girl you dated exclusively for over a year.

___ Being unjustly accused of cheating after scoring the highest grade on a chemistry test.

___ Not making the football team, a goal you've had since fourth grade.

___ Having the nickname "Larry the Cucumber" due to the size of your nose.

___ Being scoffed at by the girl you've been trying to get to notice you.

___ Losing a class election by a landslide.

___ Being laughed at in the locker room because you don't want to shower with the other boys.

___ Flunking a history test when you were thinking about becoming a history professor.

___ Forgetting your lines in a school play in front of 800 staring people.

___ Overhearing your father call you a loser because you haven't been able to find a summer job.

___ Having your pants rip when you bend over to pick something up—in front of the whole class.

Try It: Has your son suffered a wound to his spirit? Go over this checklist of "wounded spirit" symptoms and see whether you recognize any in your boy. If so, follow through on the recommendation given.

Signs of depression in children:
___ Lethargy (not wanting to get out of bed in the morning, moping around the house, showing no interest in things that normally excite him)

___ Sleep disturbances

___ Stomach complaints

___ Open anger, hostility, rage (lashing out suddenly or unexpectedly at people or things)

What to do:
"If depression is a problem for your child, it is only symptomatic of something else that is bothering him or her. Help him or her verbalize feelings. Try to anticipate the explanation for sadness, and lead the youngster into conversations that provide an opportunity to ventilate. Make yourself available to listen, without judging or belittling the feelings expressed. Simply being understood is soothing for children and adults alike."

"If the symptoms are severe or if they last more than two weeks, I urge you to…seek professional help for your son. Prolonged depression can be destructive to human beings of any age and is especially dangerous to children."

—Dr. James Dobson in *The Complete Marriage and Family Home Reference Guide* (Tyndale House)

Signs of self-hatred or deep resentment in teens:

___ Overreactions to minor frustration

___ Fear of new social situations

___ Experimentation with drugs or alcohol

___ Difficulty sleeping or eating

___ Extreme isolation and withdrawal

___ Chewing the fingernails

___ Inability to make friends

___ Disinterest in school activities

___ Bullying others

___ Threatening suicide

What to do:
"Be especially vigilant when a child who has mentioned killing himself suddenly seems carefree and happy. That sometimes means he has decided to go through with the death wish and is no longer struggling with what has been bothering him. In each of these cases, I urge you to obtain professional help for those kids. Do not console yourself with the notion that 'he'll grow out of it.' That youngster may be in desperate need of assistance. Don't miss the opportunity to provide it."

—Dr. James Dobson in the book *Bringing Up Boys* (Tyndale House)

ORIGINS OF HOMOSEXUALITY

PURPOSE: To help group members understand the origins and symptoms of gender confusion, and to equip them to identify signs of possible prehomosexuality in boys.

PASSAGES: Romans 1:25–27

PREPARATION:

- If possible, watch video 4 in advance. Approximate running time: 43 minutes. If you expect your meeting time to be short, see the Introduction to this guide for ideas on adapting the session plan.

- Make sure each person has a copy of the Participant's Guide; you may want to bring extras for visitors.

- Provide pens or pencils.

- Set up a television and video player in your meeting place.

PREVIEW:

Here's a summary of the principles in video 4:

There is a myth about homosexuality circulating today in media and schools. It is that homosexuality is genetic and can't be changed. Though no one has been able to find any evidence for this theory, TV shows and magazine articles continue to support the idea that homosexuality is determined by biology and is therefore unchangeable.

There are three facts that cast serious doubt on this theory. First, if homosexuality were genetic, it gradually would have been eliminated from the gene pool since homosexuals don't reproduce as often as heterosexuals. Second, studies show that one sibling in a set of identical twins may be homosexual while the other is not. Third, if homosexuality's origins were biological, there would be no "epidemics" of the condition such as those seen in Sodom and Gomorrah and ancient Greece.

Unfortunately, there is much confusion among parents about the subject. Many fear that their sons will turn out gay. The stories of John Paulk and Mike Haley, both of whom left the gay lifestyle through the power of Christ's love, show that change is possible and that no boy is destined at birth to be homosexual.

STEP

1

WELCOME
the group

Ask: **In what order do you think most parents would put the following items on a "wish list" for their sons?**

• **That their sons would grow up to be rich.**

• **That their sons would grow up to be famous.**

• **That their sons would grow up to be heterosexual.**

Let people vote on which items they think would be first, second, and third. Opinions will vary, depending on how the group sees "most parents."

It's likely, though, that many parents would put a high priority on their sons growing up "straight." Ask volunteers to explain why that might be. (Some answers you might hear: Parents want their children to be like them; many parents think homosexual behavior is wrong; parents don't want their kids to have to struggle with homosexuality and other people's reactions to it, etc.)

If you see signs that your son might be confused about his gender identity, what should you do?

Many parents won't know what to do. Others may suggest seeing a counselor. Still others might think homosexuality isn't a problem and can't or shouldn't be treated.

In recent years our culture has told us that we shouldn't worry if our sons enter a gay lifestyle. Many parents find themselves wondering whether they're right in wanting their sons to grow up heterosexual—and what kind of influence they can have in that area. In the following video presentation, Dr. James Dobson has some pointed things to say about raising boys who have a healthy sexual identity.

WATCH
the video

With the group, watch video segment 4, "The Origins of Homosexuality." Encourage participants to take notes in the "Video Journal" section of the Participant's Guide. Pass out pens or pencils as needed.

WRESTLE
with the principles

Discuss the video, using questions and comments along the following lines.

Which of these words best describes your feelings after watching this video: fearful, queasy, angry, or hopeful? Why?

Let volunteers respond, giving reasons for their replies if they feel comfortable doing so.

Share the following quote from Dr. Dobson's book *Bringing Up Boys*: **"If homosexuality were genetically transmitted, it would be inevitable, immutable, irresistible, and untreatable.**

Fortunately, it is not. Prevention is effective. Change is possible. Hope is available. And Christ is in the business of healing."

Note that in today's world, this is a controversial statement. But does it reflect a biblical view of homosexuality? Have the group look at Romans 1:25–27 in the "Scriptures to Study" section of the Participant's Guide and read it silently.

Then discuss the passage, using questions and comments like the following.

What are some words used in this passage to describe homosexual activity? (Shameful, unnatural, indecent, perversion.)

You may want to point out that this passage is not necessarily intended to describe the process through which every gay person becomes involved in homosexuality. **As Dr. Dobson writes in *Bringing Up Boys,* "The disorder is not typically 'chosen.' Homosexuals deeply resent being told that they selected this same-sex inclination in pursuit of sexual excitement or some other motive.... Instead, bewildered children and adolescents... find themselves dealing with something they don't even understand."**

Still, do you get the impression from these verses that homosexuality is something parents should be concerned about preventing? Why or why not? Opinions may vary, but those who care about God's view of behavior would want to help their children avoid activity He prohibits.

After wrapping up the Scripture discussion, call the group's attention to the "Apply It" section of the Participant's Guide. Thumbnail versions of these pages are at the end of the session. Depending on the size and makeup of your group, people can work on this as individuals, pairs, or teams based on the ages of participants' boys.

Allow a few minutes for this activity; then regather the group. Discuss results, using information like the following as needed.

Case Study 1:
According to Dr. Joseph Nicolosi, author of *Preventing Homosexuality: A Parent's Guide*, certain behaviors can indicate gender confusion in boys. These include a persistent desire to participate in stereotypical pastimes of girls, a strong preference

for female playmates, habitual cross-dressing, and affecting the mannerisms of a girl. Aaron may be at risk if he continues to identify exclusively with girls; his parents would be well advised to find boys with whom he can also spend time. His father or another male role model could introduce Aaron to "rough-and-tumble" games he might like. If the boy's feminine behaviors persist, his parents could have him evaluated by a counselor to determine whether he needs further help.

Case Study 2:
Tremaine may not meet his father's expectations, but the boy's behavior does not necessarily indicate gender confusion. As Dr. Nicolosi writes, "A boy can be sensitive, kind, social, artistic, gentle, and be heterosexual." If Tremaine's dad begins to appreciate his son's unique qualities, he'll be able to affirm him—thereby forming the kind of strong father-son bond that helps a boy develop a healthy sexual identity.

Case Study 3:
According to Dr. Nicolosi, feeling rejected by others because of "nonmasculine" traits can contribute to distortions in gender identity. Kyle may be vulnerable in this area. Whether this leads to "prehomosexual" behavior may depend on the influence of Kyle's new friends. He needs to find acceptance from healthy male role models, especially his father. While Kyle's parents need not take at face value the rumor regarding Kyle's friends, they should look into the matter themselves—and, if necessary, take steps to find other kids with whom Kyle can spend time.

STEP
4

WRAP UP
the session

Explain that in the next session, you'll discuss how parents, especially fathers, can cultivate healthy gender identities in their boys.

Pray for group members, thanking God for the care and concern they show for boys. Ask God to guide people in applying what they learned; if appropriate, include specific concerns that arose in discussion.

Point out the "Try It" section of the Participant's Guide. Encourage group members to use this evaluation tool at home, in preparation for addressing this issue further next time.

Apply It: What do you think the parents of these boys should do?

Case Study 1:
Aaron is three years old. Lately he's been asking his parents for a dollhouse like the one his friend Christina has. There are few boys in Aaron's neighborhood, and he plays almost exclusively with girls. When he does, he sometimes adopts a high-pitched voice that matches those of his playmates. Yesterday afternoon his mother found him trying on some of the necklaces she keeps on her dresser. "Now I'm a girl," he told her proudly. When his mother got him to give the jewelry back, he seemed "normal" again. *But for how long?* Mom wonders.

Case Study 2:
Tremaine is ten years old. His father always hoped for a son who would share his love of football, but Tremaine seems uninterested in sports of all kinds. The boy likes to spend time in the kitchen with his mother, learning to bake cakes and dice onions. He spends hours drawing pictures—and not pictures of superheroes, but of animals and sunsets. And he loves drama, relishing every chance to be in a play at school or church, reciting poems he's memorized, even singing along with characters in musicals he sees on TV. Tremaine is skinny and a bit

---

uncoordinated, but doesn't exhibit any obviously effeminate mannerisms. His dad is worried that the boy won't grow up to be "a real man."

Case Study 3:
Kyle is fifteen. He's always been shy, finding it hard to make friends. Throughout elementary school he was teased about being slightly overweight and a "bookworm." During the last year, though, he's seemed to gain acceptance from several boys at school. At first Kyle's parents were glad to hear about these kids. But then they met the boys, most of whom seem effeminate. When Kyle's folks heard a rumor from other parents that the boys were "gay," they confronted Kyle. He bristled and said, "So what if they are? A person has to be himself."

Try It: During the week, observe the boys to whom you're closest. Then react to the following statements by circling your responses. If you observe more than one boy, use a different-colored pencil to mark your responses for each.

1. I'm concerned that this boy may be confused about his gender identity.

   AGREE   DISAGREE

2. I feel confident that this boy is developing a normal masculine identity.

   AGREE   DISAGREE

3. It seems to me that this boy displays effeminate mannerisms.

   AGREE   DISAGREE

4. I'm not sure I spend enough time affirming this boy's masculinity.

   AGREE   DISAGREE

5. This boy has stated that he thinks he's gay or bisexual.

   AGREE   DISAGREE

---

6. This boy has said that he wishes he were a girl, or that he actually is a girl.

   AGREE   DISAGREE

7. This boy has shown a preference for cross-dressing.

   AGREE   DISAGREE

8. This boy needs more positive male role models.

   AGREE   DISAGREE

9. I probably need to talk with this boy about gender identity, but don't know how.

   AGREE   DISAGREE

10. This boy has a loving, respectful relationship with his father.

   AGREE   DISAGREE

PREVENTING HOMOSEXUALITY

PURPOSE: To help caregivers, especially fathers, nurture healthy gender identities in their boys by giving them affection, attention, and approval.

PASSAGES: Luke 15:11–31

PREPARATION:
- If possible, watch video 5 in advance. Approximate running time: 45 minutes. If you expect your meeting time to be short, see the Introduction to this guide for ideas on adapting the session plan.

- Make sure each person has a copy of the Participant's Guide; you may want to bring extras for visitors.

- Provide pens or pencils.

- Set up a television and video player in your meeting place.

PREVIEW: Here's a summary of the principles in video 5:

Psychologist and author Dr. Joseph Nicolosi shares findings and information from his book *Preventing Homosexuality*.

When a boy doesn't bond with a male role model early in life, the boy does not receive the special help he needs to form a healthy masculine identity. In Dr. Nicolosi's experience of counseling homosexual men, it has usually been true that the father was either absent or emotionally distant and critical of the boy—or that the mother did not "detach" from her son. During the gender identity phase, boys must be welcomed by the father and "released" by the mother. Both parents should encourage the boy to exhibit balanced, masculine traits.

Boys need to see male role models who display benevolence and strength. Boys need to know who they are, to be proud that they are becoming men. Boys also need to know they are special to their fathers, spending time together on activities that affirm their masculinity.

When a boy sees that his male role model is both good and strong and that the two of them share a masculine identity, gender confusion becomes far less likely.

STEP
1

WELCOME
the group

Say: **Last time I passed out a "Try It" sheet to help you evaluate whether your boys might be struggling with gender confusion. I won't ask you to reveal whether you did the exercise or what you found out. Instead, I'm going to read the statements that were on the sheet and ask you to respond with a silent "agree" or "disagree," based on what you know of one of the boys in your care.**

Give group members time to think about their reactions to each of the following.

1. **I'm concerned that this boy may be confused about his gender identity.**

2. **I feel confident that this boy is developing a normal masculine identity.**

3. It seems to me that this boy displays effeminate mannerisms.

4. I'm not sure I spend enough time affirming this boy's masculinity.

5. This boy has stated that he thinks he's gay or bisexual.

6. This boy has said that he wishes he were a girl, or that he actually is a girl.

7. This boy has shown a preference for cross-dressing.

8. This boy needs more positive male role models.

9. I probably need to talk with this boy about gender identity, but don't know how.

10. This boy has a loving, respectful relationship with his father.

After finishing the list, say: **Whether or not you see signs of gender confusion in the boy you were thinking of, chances are that you want to do all you can to help him grow up with a healthy sexual identity. In today's video segment, Dr. James Dobson and clinical psychologist Dr. Joseph Nicolosi, an authority on the prevention and treatment of homosexuality, tell us more about how to do that.**

WATCH
the video

With the group, watch video segment 5, "Preventing Homosexuality." Encourage participants to take notes in the "Video Journal" section of the Participant's Guide. Pass out pens or pencils as needed.

WRESTLE
with the principles

Discuss the video, using questions and comments along the following lines.

If you had to summarize the message of this video in three words, how would you do it?

There's no single right answer to this question, of course; affirm all the replies you can. Then offer the following thoughts.

In his book *Preventing Homosexuality: A Parent's Guide,* Dr. Joseph Nicolosi points out that boys need from their fathers "the three *A*'s": affection, attention, and approval. Boys who don't get these three things, and who fail to "detach" from their mothers at an early age and identify with their fathers, can suffer gender confusion.

Let's look at the story of a father who gave his son "the three *A*'s."

Have group members read Luke 15:11–31, the parable of the prodigal son, in the "Scriptures to Study" section of the Participant's Guide. Discuss the passage, using questions and comments like the following.

How did the father show affection to his son? (By hugging and kissing him.)

How did the father give the son attention? (By listening to his request for a share of the estate.)

How did the father show the son approval, despite what the son had done? (Without approving the son's rebellion and foolishness, the father celebrated the young man's return because he valued him as a son.)

What was the older brother's reaction? (He was jealous of the attention paid to his "undeserving" brother.)

What could this tell us about the older son's needs? (He needed "the three *A*'s," too. In verses 31 and 32 the father does affirm the older son.)

After wrapping up the Scripture discussion, have group members look at the "Apply It" section of the Participant's Guide. Thumbnail versions of these pages are at the end of the session. Have people work on this individually, responding to the portions that apply to them.

Allow a few minutes for this activity; then regather the group. Discuss results, using questions and comments like the following.

What do you think of the quote from Dr. Nicolosi? What conclusions do you draw from it?

Responses will vary. One possible conclusion is that lacking a loving, respectful relationship with one's father increases the risk of gender confusion.

As you discuss the sections of the sheet addressed to fathers, married moms, and single moms, consider the following.

For fathers:
Let volunteers respond, but don't press. Dads may be uncomfortable admitting shortcomings in these areas—especially any involving painful childhood memories about their own fathers.

For married moms:
Encourage moms to tell "success stories" about their husbands, rather than embarrassing the men by dwelling on failures. Urge spouses to talk later about suggestions for improvement in these areas.

For single moms:
Participants in this category may express frustration over the difficulty of finding good male role models. If time allows, ask the group to suggest ways of finding such men in your group or church. Encourage men in the group to consider offering help in this area.

Summarize by urging people to see a counselor if they're concerned that their boys might be struggling with gender confusion or prehomosexual behavior. Share this advice from Dr. Dobson's book *Bringing Up Boys*:

"Be very careful whom you consult, however. Getting the wrong advice at this stage could be most unfortunate, solidifying the tendencies that are developing. Given the direction the mental-health profession has gone, most secular psychiatrists, psychologists, and counselors would, I believe, take the wrong approach—telling your child that he is homosexual and needs to accept that fact....You *do* need to accept the child and affirm his worth regardless of the characteristics you observe

but also work patiently with a therapist in redirecting those tendencies....Sometimes a visit with a professional is needed just to determine whether or not a child is at risk."

WRAP UP
the session

Call attention to the "Try It" section of the Participant's Guide. Encourage fathers and single moms to act on the practical suggestions found there.

Close by praying for the fathers represented in your group, asking God to help them give affection, attention, and approval to their sons. Pray, too, that the Lord will enable single moms to find the right male role models for their boys.

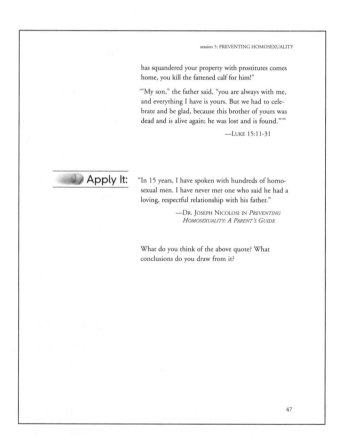

session 5: PREVENTING HOMOSEXUALITY

has squandered your property with prostitutes comes home, you kill the fattened calf for him!'

"'My son,' the father said, 'you are always with me, and everything I have is yours. But we had to celebrate and be glad, because this brother of yours was dead and is alive again; he was lost and is found.'"

—LUKE 15:11-31

Apply It: "In 15 years, I have spoken with hundreds of homosexual men. I have never met one who said he had a loving, respectful relationship with his father."

—DR. JOSEPH NICOLOSI IN *PREVENTING HOMOSEXUALITY: A PARENT'S GUIDE*

What do you think of the above quote? What conclusions do you draw from it?

47

For fathers:

To help boys develop healthy masculine identities, fathers need to give their boys the three *A*'s: Affection, Attention, and Approval.

On a scale of 1 to 10 (10 being best), rate yourself and your own father in the following areas:

	YOU	YOUR FATHER
Showing son affection		
Giving son attention		
Showing son approval		

For married moms:

Try to come up with an example of something your husband has done (or could do) in each of the following areas:

Showing son affection

Giving son attention

Showing son approval

For single moms:

Indicate whether you think your son has a trustworthy male role model in his life to perform the following functions:

	YES	NO
Showing son affection		
Giving son attention		
Showing son approval		

 **Try It:** *For dads:*

Showing AFFECTION to your son

In addition to expressing affection in words, try some of these:

- Hug
- Arm around the shoulders
- Handshake
- Pat on the knee
- Back scratch
- Kiss on the cheek, forehead, or top of the head
- Pat on the back
- High-five
- Quick stroke of the hair
- Shoulder massage
- Wrestling

Giving ATTENTION to your son

When you're listening to your son, avoid "multitasking." For example, don't try to read the paper or watch TV with one eye while he's telling you about his day.

Body language is important, too. Lean forward, making positive eye contact. Nod occasionally to show you're eager to hear what your son has to say. Slumping in your chair, folding your arms across your chest, or staring to one side of the speaker indicates you're not interested.

Showing APPROVAL to your son

Here are three ways to show approval:

1. Praise your son to someone else within your son's hearing. Tell others what you like about your son—not just good grades or tennis skills, but also character traits.

2. Tuck a complimentary note into a lunch sack or binder—even a message as short as "I'm proud of you."

3. Catch him doing something right, and mention it. For example, "I noticed you showed mercy to your sister when you complimented her new haircut instead of making a joke about it." Or, "I saw you pick up the little boy down the street when he fell off his scooter. I can tell you care about people."

—ADAPTED FROM *PARENTS' GUIDE TO THE SPIRITUAL MENTORING OF TEENS* (TYNDALE HOUSE)

For single moms:

Finding a Male Role Model for Your Son

"To every single mom who is on this quest, let me emphasize first that you have an invaluable resource in our heavenly Father. He created your children and they are precious to Him. How do I know that? Because he said repeatedly in His Word that He has a special tenderness for fatherless children and their mothers. There are many references in Scripture to their plight [see Deuteronomy 10:17–18; 27:19; Psalm 68:5; Zechariah 7:10]."

"[The Lord] is waiting for you to ask Him for help. I have seen miraculous answers to prayer on behalf of those who have sought His help in what seemed like impossible situations."

"Make an all-out effort to find a father-substitute for your boys. An uncle or a neighbor or a coach or a musical director or a Sunday school teacher may do the trick. Placing your boys under the influence of such a man for even a single hour per week can make a great difference. Get them involved in Boy Scouts, Boy's Club, soccer, or Little League. Check out Big Brothers as a possibility. Give your boys biographies, and take them to movies or rent videos that focus on strong masculine (but moral) heroes. However you choose to solve the problem, do not let the years go by without a man's influence in the lives of your boys."

—DR. JAMES DOBSON IN THE BOOK *BRINGING UP BOYS* (TYNDALE HOUSE)

session 6

ROUTINE PANIC

PURPOSE: To help participants evaluate how busyness may be hindering their ability to raise their boys effectively.

PASSAGES: Luke 10:38–42

PREPARATION:
- If possible, watch video 6 in advance. Approximate running time: 41 minutes. If you expect your meeting time to be short, see the Introduction to this guide for ideas on adapting the session plan.

- Make sure each person has a copy of the Participant's Guide; you may want to bring extras for visitors.

- Provide pens or pencils.

- Set up a television and video player in your meeting place.

PREVIEW: Here's a summary of the principles in video 6:

Fathers are vital in raising boys because of their role as modelers of masculinity. A father needs to teach his son four things to prepare him for having his own family someday: to be the provider, the protector, the leader, and the spiritual mentor.

Unfortunately, this often doesn't happen—due in part to what Dr. Dobson calls "routine panic."

Routine panic may be the greatest source of difficulty in the American family today. Many parents are overworked and exhausted, and their sense of community has broken down. Studies show a lower incidence of rebellion and difficulty with children when the family spends time together. Young children who spend long hours in day care have displayed three times more behavior problems than those who don't. And boys especially need the stability that time with parents can provide.

Parents must reserve more time for their kids. Not every household can opt out of the two-income work schedule that consumes so many hours for so many families, but those who can should consider the benefits.

S T E P
1

WELCOME
the group

Ask: **If I could give you a big box of parenting help today, would you want the box to contain motivation, money, or time?**

Some may quickly answer, "Time," while others might want money in order to buy time.

Then ask: **Why? What is so difficult about finding time to parent?** (I have too much to do; the kids have too much home-work; by the time I get home from work it's time to put the kids to bed, etc.)

In today's video, Dr. James Dobson has some things to say about the importance of fathers and mothers spending time with their boys—and the problem of finding that time.

WATCH
the video

With the group, watch video segment 6, "Routine Panic." Encourage participants to take notes in the "Video Journal" section of the Participant's Guide. Pass out pens or pencils as needed.

WRESTLE
with the principles

Discuss the video, using questions and comments along the following lines.

Why is it especially important for moms and dads to spend time with their boys? (For one thing, boys seem to get into more trouble than girls do when left unattended.)

Which do you think is more vital: giving kids "quality" time or "quantity" time? Opinions may vary, but it's hard to argue with the idea that children need both—and that a tiny amount of "quality" time would be no more satisfying than a tiny amount of "quality" steak in a restaurant.

Does the term "routine panic" apply to your life? If so, how? Encourage people to be specific.

Have the group turn to the "Scriptures to Study" section of the Participant's Guide. Read Luke 10:38–42. Then discuss the passage, using questions and comments like the following.

Why was Martha frustrated? (She had so much to do, and Mary wasn't helping.)

If Martha were a mom today, what kinds of things might be keeping her busy? (Helping kids with schoolwork, making lunches, driving kids to soccer games, perhaps working outside the home, etc.)

What do you think Jesus meant by His response to Martha? (Probably that most of Martha's concerns weren't as important as the opportunity to spend time with Him.)

If you were Martha, how would you respond to what Jesus said? (Some possibilities: "But how will all this work get done?" "That's not fair!" Or one might let the chores go and join Mary at the feet of Jesus.)

If Jesus dropped by your house and saw "routine panic" there, what do you think He would say? (He might urge us to worry less and trust Him more [I Peter 5:7]; He might challenge our assumptions about how many things "must" get done.)

What "one thing" do you think Jesus would want you to concentrate on when it comes to raising your boys? Why?

Answers will vary. One possibility: Raising boys in a way that reinforces their relationship with God. Affirm as many replies as you can.

Then call attention to the "Apply It" section of the Participant's Guide. Thumbnail versions of these pages are at the end of the session. Let people read and react to the quotes. Discuss reactions, using questions like the following.

Quote 1:
How do your boys benefit from the time you spend at work? How might the amount of time you spend working be a negative factor in their lives? At what point do the negatives outweigh the positives?

Quote 2:
Is "family time" typical in your home? How do you think it's affecting the boys in your care? Do you schedule "focused" family time? If so, how has that worked out?

Quote 3:
Do you identify with the majority of women in this survey? Why or why not? If most women actually became homemakers, how might it affect the way boys are raised?

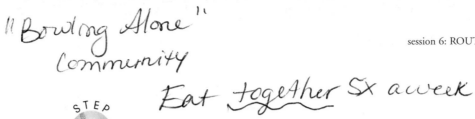

"Bowling Alone"
Community

Eat together 5x a week

STEP 4

WRAP UP
the session

Explain that in the next session you'll explore how finding time for boys can help solve a variety of questions parents and grandparents ask.

If possible, have people pray for each other, especially regarding specific time pressures they face.

In closing, point out the "Try It" section of the Participant's Guide. Encourage group members to keep track of the "quantity" and "quality" time they spend with their boys this week—not to spur guilt feelings, but as a first step toward making the most of family time.

DR. JAMES DOBSON'S bringing up boys

Scriptures to Study

"As Jesus and His disciples were on their way, He came to a village where a woman named Martha opened her home to Him. She had a sister called Mary, who sat at the Lord's feet listening to what He said. But Martha was distracted by all the preparations that had to be made. She came to Him and asked, 'Lord, don't You care that my sister has left me to do the work by myself? Tell her to help me!'

"'Martha, Martha,' the Lord answered, 'you are worried and upset about many things, but only one thing is needed. Mary has chosen what is better, and it will not be taken away from her.'"

—LUKE 10:38–42

 Apply It: With which of the following quotes, taken from Dr. Dobson's book *Bringing Up Boys*, do you most identify? Why?

QUOTE 1
"Americans…are already the most vacation-starved people in the industrialized world, with an average of thirteen vacation days per year, compared with twenty-five or more in Japan, Canada, Britain, Germany, and Italy. The study revealed that 32 percent of those surveyed said they work and eat lunch at the same time, and another 32 percent said they never leave the building once they arrive at work. Some 34 percent said they have such pressing jobs that they have no breaks or downtime while on the job. Nineteen percent

say their job makes them feel older than they are, and 17 percent say work causes them to lose sleep at night. Seventeen percent said it is difficult to take time off or leave work even in an emergency, and 8 percent said they believe if they were to become seriously ill, they would be fired or demoted." (*Business Wire*, February 21, 2001)

QUOTE 2
"It is becoming less common these days for a teenager to have time isolated for focused interaction with family members. Most of the time they spend with their family is what you might call 'family and time': family and TV, family and dinner, family and homework, etc. The lives of each family member are usually so jam-packed that the opportunity to spend time together doing unique activities—talking about life, visiting special places, playing games, and sharing spiritual explorations—has to be scheduled in advance. Few do so." (George Barna, *Generation Next* [Regal Books, 1995])

QUOTE 3
"According to a recent survey by Youth Intelligence, a market research and trend-tracking firm in New York, 68 percent of 3,000 married and single young women said they'd ditch work if they could afford to. And a Cosmo poll of 800 women revealed the same startling statistic: two out of three respondents would rather kick back *a casa* than climb the corporate ladder. 'It's no fleeting fantasy'—these women honestly aspire to the domestic life, and many will follow through with it,' says Jane Buckingham, president of Youth Intelligence." (Judy Dutton, "Meet the New Housewife Wanna-bes," *Cosmopolitan*, June 2000)

56

57

51

DR. JAMES DOBSON'S bringing up boys

Try It: This week, try keeping track of the quantity and quality of time you spend with your boys. You may be surprised at the results. If you're caring for more than one boy, make a copy of this sheet for each one.

	Quantity of time spent	*Quality of time spent* (Describe what you did and the effect you think it had on the boy)
Sunday		
Monday		
Tuesday		
Wednesday		
Thursday		
Friday		
Saturday		

58

session 7

QUESTIONS FROM PARENTS & GRANDPARENTS

PURPOSE: To help participants deal with a variety of boy-raising challenges by finding more time to parent.

PASSAGES: Luke 12:22-31

PREPARATION:
- If possible, watch video 7 in advance. Approximate running time: 46 minutes. If you expect your meeting time to be short, see the Introduction to this guide for ideas on adapting the session plan.

- Make sure each person has a copy of the Participant's Guide; you may want to bring extras for visitors.

- Provide pens or pencils.

- Set up a television and video player in your meeting place.

PREVIEW: In this segment, Dr. Dobson fields questions from the audience. Participants ask advice on a variety of topics related to raising boys.

WELCOME
the group

Say: **Last time I encouraged you to keep track of the time you spent with your boys. How many were able to do that?**

Chances are that some group members didn't complete the exercise. If that's the case, give people a few moments to come up with a guess at the average amount of time they spent with their boys per day since your last meeting.

If participants want to volunteer how much time they spent, let them—but to avoid embarrassing those who fear they don't "measure up," don't ask.

How do you feel about the amount of time you spent? Why?

If you kept track, were there any surprises? Was your actual time greater or less than you thought it would be?

What kinds of things stood in the way of spending time with your boy?

What's an example of some "quality" time you spent with your boy? What effect do you think it had on the boy? On you?

In today's video segment, Dr. James Dobson answers questions from parents and grandparents about raising boys. Let's see how many of those questions could be answered in part by finding more time to parent.

WATCH
the video

With the group, watch video segment 7, "Questions from Parents and Grandparents." Encourage participants to take notes in the "Video Journal" section of the Participant's Guide. Pass out pens or pencils as needed.

STEP

WRESTLE
with the principles

Discuss the video, using questions and comments along the following lines.

With which questions did you most identify?

Which of Dr. Dobson's recommendations do you think would take the most time to follow?

How would you respond to a parent or grandparent who says in frustration, "That's great advice, but where can I find the time to do it?"

After listening to ideas, say: **Following even the best advice takes time. As we discussed in our last session, many parents can't seem to find enough hours in the day. Let's see if we can do anything about that.**

Direct the group's attention to the "Scriptures to Study" section of the Participant's Guide. Read Luke 12:22–31. Then discuss the passage, using questions and comments like the following.

What does this say a parent should seek first? (God's kingdom.) How can parents do that? (By making His priorities theirs; by passing on godly values to their children; by valuing their kids more than possessions, etc.)

What worries tend to keep us from spending time with our kids? (That we won't have enough money if we don't work as hard or as much; that people will think less of us if our homes are messy; that our possessions will fall apart if we don't maintain them, etc.)

What's the hardest thing for you about obeying Jesus' teaching here?

Read the following quote from Dr. Dobson's book: **"The harried lifestyle that characterizes most Westerners leads not only to the isolation of people from each other in the wider community. It is also the primary reason for the breakdown of the family. Husbands and wives don't have time for each other and** many of them hardly know their children. They don't get together with relatives, friends, or neighbors because they are tyrannized by a never-ending 'to do' list. Repeatedly during my research in writing this book…I came face-to-face with the same sad phenomenon. Parents were simply too distracted and exhausted to protect and care for their children."

What can we do? Let's consider some options.

Have people work individually on the "Apply It" section of the Participant's Guide. Give group members time to circle their answers. Then discuss the results, using questions and comments like the following.

What things did you think you could change this week?

Which ones will take some time to work out?

Are there any you wish you could do, but that seem impossible? Encourage group members to put these on their lists of things to pray about this week. If possible, let volunteers share other parental time-saving tips from their own experience.

WRAP UP
the session

Explain that in the next session you'll be taking a look at boys' self-images and some ways in which their identities are frequently undermined.

If possible, have group members pray for each other, especially regarding specific time pressures they face.

In closing, call attention to the "Try It" section of the Participant's Guide. Explain that the activities suggested there are not assignments—they're ideas for getting the most out of brief times spent with boys.

Apply It: Which of the following changes might make your lifestyle less hectic—and give you more time to parent? Circle your responses.

1. Watching less TV.
- This would help, and I can start this week
- This would help, but I'll need time to work out the details
- This would help, but there's no way it can happen
- This probably wouldn't help even if I did it

2. Going from a two-income household to one income.
- This would help, and I can start this week
- This would help, but I'll need time to work out the details
- This would help, but there's no way it can happen
- This probably wouldn't help even if I did it

3. Working at home.
- This would help, and I can start this week
- This would help, but I'll need time to work out the details
- This would help, but there's no way it can happen
- This probably wouldn't help even if I did it

4. Spending less time on hobbies or recreation.
- This would help, and I can start this week
- This would help, but I'll need time to work out the details
- This would help, but there's no way it can happen
- This probably wouldn't help even if I did it

5. Getting a slower wristwatch.
- This would help, and I can start this week
- This would help, but I'll need time to work out the details
- This would help, but there's no way it can happen
- This probably wouldn't help even if I did it

6. Getting a job with a shorter commute.
- This would help, and I can start this week
- This would help, but I'll need time to work out the details
- This would help, but there's no way it can happen
- This probably wouldn't help even if I did it

7. Postponing a goal (getting a degree, remodeling the house, etc.).
- This would help, and I can start this week
- This would help, but I'll need time to work out the details
- This would help, but there's no way it can happen
- This probably wouldn't help even if I did it

8. Getting rid of some possessions so I don't have to spend time maintaining them.
- This would help, and I can start this week
- This would help, but I'll need time to work out the details
- This would help, but there's no way it can happen
- This probably wouldn't help even if I did it

9. Reducing my work hours.
- This would help, and I can start this week
- This would help, but I'll need time to work out the details
- This would help, but there's no way it can happen
- This probably wouldn't help even if I did it

10. Better managing the time I do have.
- This would help, and I can start this week
- This would help, but I'll need time to work out the details
- This would help, but there's no way it can happen
- This probably wouldn't help even if I did it

Try It: This week, try setting aside a short "sabbath" time each day to spend one-on-one with your son. Use the following ideas to get you thinking about refreshing, renewing things to do together.

Preschool:
Sunday: Hide pennies around your home and have a treasure hunt.

Monday: Play "volleyballoon" by batting a balloon back and forth over a net made of tied-together plastic bags.

Tuesday: Make snakes with modeling clay or dough.

Wednesday: Sit in a darkened room, listen carefully, and see how many separate sounds you can identify.

Thursday: Cut out pictures from old magazines to give you ideas of things to pray about.

Friday: Build a fort out of blankets and chairs and take a nap in it.

Saturday: Have a "pretend picnic" on a blanket on the floor.

Elementary:
Sunday: Make pizza or ice cream sundaes and let your boy choose the toppings.

Monday: Get two books of jokes or riddles from the library and take turns reading them to each other.

Tuesday: Make up obstacle courses and time each other as you navigate them. This can be done outdoors (run to the tree, hop on one foot to the fence, then come back and give me five) or indoors (touch that wall, get a napkin from the kitchen, and return while flapping your arms and reciting the alphabet backward).

Wednesday: Tell each other how your day might have been different if you could have seen Jesus with you wherever you went.

Thursday: Turn cupcakes into spiders by adding legs made of pipe cleaners or toothpicks.

Friday: Play a favorite board game, but let your boy change the rules.

Saturday: Try using the wrong equipment for a sport. For example, use a tennis ball to shoot baskets, or a table tennis paddle and beanbag to play baseball.

Adolescence:

Sunday: Rent a video of an old movie that looks especially dull. Watch it together with the sound off, making up dialogue as you go.

Monday: Play "Can you top this?" with the weirdest, most embarrassing, most frustrating, most boring, and funniest events of your day.

Tuesday: Look over the calendar for the next month and draw a star on each day that either of you might be under more stress than usual. Plan to pray for each other on those days.

Wednesday: Ask your son to help you memorize a passage of Scripture, using any method he thinks will work.

Thursday: Go through your home and take turns snapping photos of the things you consider most valuable. Be sure to take pictures of each other before you're finished.

Friday: Ask your son's advice about a problem you face at work, or his opinion about a change you'd like to make in your household routine.

Saturday: Go to the market together and let your boy pick out the food and beverage for supper. The catch: Everything has to be the same color.

session 8

MEN R FOOLS

PURPOSE: To help group members protect boys from the effects of antimale messages often found in the mass media.

PASSAGES: Genesis 1:27, 31; 1 Timothy 3:8–11; 5:1–2

PREPARATION:
- If possible, watch video 8 in advance. Approximate running time: 46 minutes. If you expect your meeting time to be short, see the Introduction to this guide for ideas on adapting the session plan.

- Make sure each person has a copy of the Participant's Guide; you may want to bring extras for visitors.

- Provide pens or pencils.

- Set up a television and video player in your meeting place.

PREVIEW: Here's a summary of the principles in video 8:

"Male chauvinist pigs" is a term descriptive of the anger evident in the 1960s when Valeria Solanis formed the Society for Cutting Up Men, SCUM. Feminism may be less flamboyant today, but hatred of men is still alive on some university campuses in women's study programs. Disrespect for men has become politically correct. This is highly relevant to raising boys because it can influence the way a boy comes to see masculinity in general and himself in particular.

TV commercials illustrate this bias, expressing disapproval of men through disrespectful and degrading humor. The formula is to portray men as stupid, often overweight, balding, and slovenly. Advertising companies spend millions of dollars on these messages—and they work, perhaps because men don't seem to see that the joke is on them.

WELCOME
the group

Start by reading the following descriptions of characters that might be seen on TV. After each description, ask which of the characters are probably male, and which are probably female.

1. This character literally drools over a person of the opposite sex.

2. This character has bad table manners.

3. This character is physically abused by a spouse.

4. This character is smart, but has to play dumb to attract the opposite sex.

5. This character oppresses the opposite sex.

6. This character is insensitive to the needs of the opposite sex.

7. This character is strong but stupid.

8. This character is violent.

9. **This character is a perpetual adolescent, refusing to grow up.**

10. **This character refuses to help with housework.**

Opinions will vary, but it's likely that all answers will be "male" except (3) and (4). Ask: **What do you think your boys have learned from TV about what it means to be male?**

Answers will vary. You may want to point out that boys tend to watch and identify with action heroes and sports figures, who might be seen as positive role models. Yet many of the males depicted on TV are anything but admirable—bumbling, over-sexed, violent, boorish, insensitive. Girls and women, on the other hand, are often idealized.

In the following video, Dr. James Dobson takes a look at the impact of popular media today and their not-so-subtle messages to boys.

WATCH
the video

Watch video segment 8, "Men R Fools." Encourage participants to take notes in the "Video Journal" section of the Participant's Guide. Pass out pens or pencils as needed.

WRESTLE
with the principles

Discuss the video, using questions and comments along the following lines.

According to the point of view often presented in the popular media, why do men need to be "fixed"? (Because they are dummies, insensitive, inferior, out-of-control, childish, etc.)

What do you think would happen if the popular media more often portrayed men as strong and honorable?
Opinions will vary. Some might think women would be short-changed, or that the media would be less entertaining. Others

61

might think it would encourage boys to see themselves as capable, and to respect themselves.

Have people read Genesis 1:27, 31 in the "Scriptures to Study" section of the Participant's Guide. Ask: **What does God think of the male gender He created?** (He saw His whole creation, including male and female, as "very good.")

Why do you suppose so many people throughout history have seen one gender as good and the other as less than good? (Ego; wanting power over others; prejudice; fear; valuing one trait [physical strength or nurturing, for example] over another; reacting to real or imagined slights by the opposite sex, etc.)

Have a volunteer read 1 Timothy 3:8–11. Then discuss, using questions and comments like the following.

According to Paul, what things make people worthy of respect? (Sincerity, temperance, integrity, trustworthiness, etc.)

So which gender is worthy of respect? (Both, according to this passage, depending on the character of the individuals.)

Have a volunteer read 1 Timothy 5:1–2. Discuss, using questions and comments like the following.

If everyone adopted this view, what would happen to the "battle of the sexes"? (It might not take place.)

Why? (There might be more mutual respect.)

Read the following quote from Dr. Dobson's book *Bringing Up Boys*: **"[Boys] are the victims of a long and costly battle between the sexes that has vilified the essence of masculinity and ripped into the world of children. And that is not good. Pitting boys and girls against each other as competitors and enemies cannot be healthy for anyone!"**

Explain that the following exercise is designed to help group members evaluate how this "battle of the sexes," as commonly portrayed on TV, might influence their boys. Be sure to mention that you are not endorsing these programs, this is simply an encouragement to think critically.

Direct attention to the "Apply It" section of the Participant's Guide. Thumbnail versions of these pages are at the end of the session. Allow people to work on this individually or in pairs. After a few minutes, regather and share results.

Answers will vary, but you may want to point out that many of the husbands are portrayed as lovable bumblers (Homer, Doug, Ray, Herman, Hank). Their appetites for food and/or sex are sometimes out of control (Homer, Doug, Ray, Gomez). The men are often more befuddled and have less insight than their wives (Homer, Doug, Ray, Cliff, Greg, Herman, Hank, Gomez). It's interesting to note that the two oldest series listed *(I Love Lucy, Leave It to Beaver)* featured more capable husbands.

Ask: **Why do you suppose there are few Ward Cleavers on television anymore?**

What ideas might a boy get from a steady diet of today's sitcoms? (He might come to believe he's inferior to girls, or that it's okay to be immature, insensitive, hedonistic, or irresponsible.)

As adults we may be able to see through the messages in the media. But our boys may need help to question the "Men R Fools" theme they're likely to encounter. Today's "Try It" activity can assist us with that.

STEP
4

WRAP UP
the session

Next time, we'll consider how to teach boys to respect themselves and the opposite sex.

Pray for the group. As appropriate, mention specific concerns that were brought up.

Point out the "Try It" section of the Participant's Guide. **Here are some ways to help a boy take a closer look at positive and negative role models.** If you have extra time, encourage group members to read through the activities and think about possible ways to use them during the week.

"Do not rebuke an older man harshly, but exhort him as if he were your father. Treat younger men as brothers, older women as mothers, and younger women as sisters, with absolute purity."

—1 TIMOTHY 3:8–11; 5:1–2

Apply It: Compare and contrast the following TV husbands and wives. Who's smarter? Who's more mature? Who's out of control? If you aren't familiar with all the shows, try to come up with other examples.

The Simpsons: Homer vs. Marge

The King of Queens: Doug vs. Carrie

Everybody Loves Raymond: Ray vs. Debra

The Cosby Show: Cliff vs. Clair

Dharma and Greg: Greg vs. Dharma

The Munsters: Herman vs. Lily

King of the Hill: Hank vs. Peggy

70

The Addams Family: Gomez vs. Morticia

I Love Lucy: Ricky vs. Lucy

Leave It to Beaver: Ward vs. June

Try It: *Preschool:*
Look together through the comics pages of the newspaper. Have your son draw a circle around each boy and man portrayed. Ask: Is this guy smart or silly? How is he like a real-life boy or man? How is he different? Do the boys and men in the comics seem dumber than the girls and ladies? Assure your son that even if the comics tend to make fun of "dopey" dads and "rude" boys, and even if girls and ladies in the comics are often the "wise" and "normal" ones, there's nothing wrong with being a real-life boy.

Elementary:
View a few TV sitcoms, cartoons, or commercials together (if you're not sure they'll be appropriate, tape them in advance and pre-screen them). Have your son watch for the ways in which boys and men are portrayed, especially compared to the depiction of female characters. Is it true that male characters are much more likely to be clueless, sloppy, insensitive, dim-witted, crude, and selfish? How does your son feel about that? Explain that no matter how guys are depicted on TV,

71

there's no reason to be embarrassed about being one— and that we can find much better male role models in places like the Bible.

Adolescence:
Choose a man you admire, perhaps a nearby relative or a friend from church, and arrange to have lunch with him and your son. During the conversation, point out some of the qualities you admire in this man. Ask him to explain who some of *his* male role models were. Don't turn the lunch into a lecture; just let the man be an example to your son of what a male can and should be.

72

session 9

BOYS R FOOLS, TOO

PURPOSE: To help group members raise boys to respect both themselves and the opposite sex.

PASSAGES: Ephesians 5:33; 1 Peter 3:7

PREPARATION:
- If possible, watch video 9 in advance. Approximate running time: 46 minutes. If you expect your meeting time to be short, see the Introduction to this guide for ideas on adapting the session plan.

- Make sure each person has a copy of the Participant's Guide; you may want to bring extras for visitors.

- Provide pens or pencils.

- Set up a television and video player in your meeting place.

PREVIEW: Here's a summary of the principles in video 9:

Men are being disrespected and humiliated in our culture, not only in TV commercials but also in literature, greeting cards, sitcoms, and movies. For example, the film *Runaway Bride* manipulates the audience by reversing sex roles. The woman is in control, the man is submissive. The pattern tells men—and boys—they deserve to be made fun of, to be made fools.

Our culture's message rips through the heart of the relationship between a man and a woman. Boys are left confused, with no idea of what it means to be a man. Without good role models, they are left vulnerable to attacks by this bias.

Conventional wisdom says girls are treated unfairly in school, yet boys are the ones in trouble. Funds have been taken from boys' activities and given to girls' programs. While the "girl power" movement tries to compensate for prejudice against girls, boys continue to flounder. Because boys can't defend themselves, parents and youth organizations need to step in to celebrate the masculine gender and meet the special needs of boys as well as girls.

STEP
1

WELCOME
the group

Begin by having men and women sit on opposite sides of the room. Tell them you're going to have a "Battle of the Sexes," and encourage them to show some "gender loyalty."

Read aloud the following list of activities. After each activity, ask group members to vote on which gender is better at performing it. If yours is a quiet group, let people vote with a show of hands; if group members are rambunctious, have them yell out their choices.

1. Driving

2. Sewing

3. Playing basketball

4. **Disciplining children**

5. **Cooking**

6. **Conversation**

7. **Climbing trees**

8. **Channel surfing**

9. **Nuclear physics**

10. **Vacuuming the floor**

Opinions will vary. If some group members refuse to vote, saying that neither sex is consistently better at an activity, that's fine. Just follow up with questions like these:

Are the boys you know warriors in the "Battle of the Sexes"? If so, how do they express this? (Some possibilities: "Boys are better than girls!" "Girls have cooties!" "No girls allowed!" "You throw like a girl!")

If there's a war between the genders, which one do you think has the advantage these days? Why?

In such a "warlike" atmosphere, how do you teach boys to respect the opposite sex as well as respecting themselves?

Affirm as many answers as you can. Then introduce the video as follows.

Let's watch as Dr. James Dobson has more to say about biases against boys—and the need for the sexes to respect each other.

STEP
2

WATCH
the video

Watch video segment 9, "Boys R Fools, Too." Encourage participants to take notes in the "Video Journal" section of the Participant's Guide. Pass out pens or pencils as needed.

STEP
3

WRESTLE
with the principles

Discuss the video, using questions and comments along the following lines.

What do you think boys are likely to learn from the entertainment and news media about the following?

- **How to treat a girl on a date**

- **Whether boys are as smart as girls**

- **Whether to have sex before marriage**

- **Whether a man has responsibilities as family provider, protector, and spiritual leader**

Opinions will vary. Then ask:

What do you think boys are likely to learn in a public school about these issues?

Again, answers will vary. Challenge the group:

If our boys aren't likely to gain a biblical worldview on these subjects at school or in the media, what can we do?

Some participants may be interested in changing the media and schools; others may point out the need for parents and churches to teach boys about their roles and about mutual respect between the sexes.

Have a volunteer read Ephesians 5:33 from the "Scriptures to Study" section of the Participant's Guide. Ask:

According to this verse, who deserves more love—men or women? (Neither. Husbands are to love their wives as they love themselves.)

How does this passage contrast with the view that males should be ashamed of their masculine tendencies? (It assumes that men will love themselves; in fact, verse 29 implies that self-hate isn't normal.)

What does this verse say about respect between the sexes?
(It instructs wives to respect their husbands.)

Does that mean men don't have to respect women?

To answer that question, have the group read 1 Peter 3:7 from the Participant's Guide.

How are husbands to treat their wives? (With consideration and respect.)

What's this about the "weaker partner"? Is that disrespectful toward women? (No; it's probably a reference to physical strength.)

How would you summarize what these two verses have to say about the relationship between the sexes? Answers will vary, but most people are likely to point out the need for mutual respect, love, and sensitivity to the lesser physical strength of women.

How can we apply these ideas to our boys today? Let's find out.

Direct attention to the "Apply It" section of the Participant's Guide. Thumbnail versions of these pages are at the end of the session. Let people work on this individually. Then regather the group to share results. Discuss, using questions like the following.

Which of these principles do you think is most important to teach a boy? Why?

Which principles would you not teach your boy? Why?

Which might be easiest to teach? Hardest? Why?

Which of these principles are widely accepted in our culture today? Which aren't?

At what age do you think these principles should be taught? Why?

How do you feel about your progress in teaching these concepts? What progress would you like to make in the next year?

S T E P
4

WRAP UP
the session

In the next session, we'll hear more questions and answers on the subject of bringing up boys.

Pray for the group. As appropriate, mention specific concerns that were brought up.

Call attention to the "Try It" section of the Participant's Guide. **Here are some ways to teach the principles we've been talking about.** Encourage group members to use one or two of the activities during the week—or to come up with their own.

Apply It:

If you speak disparagingly of the opposite sex, or if you refer to females as sex objects, those attitudes will translate directly into dating and marital relationships later on. Remember that your goal is to prepare a boy to lead a family when he's grown and to show him how to earn the respect of those he serves.

1. Tell him it is great to laugh and have fun with his friends, but advise him not to be "goofy." Guys who are goofy are not respected, and people, especially girls and women, do not follow boys and men whom they disrespect.

____ I've taught this principle.

____ I don't agree with this principle.

____ I hope to teach this principle.

____ I agree with this principle,
    but don't think I could teach it.

2. Also, tell your son that he is never to hit a girl under any circumstances. Remind him that she is not as strong as he is and that she is deserving of his respect.

____ I've taught this principle.

____ I don't agree with this principle.

____ I hope to teach this principle.

____ I agree with this principle,
    but don't think I could teach it.

---

3. Not only should he not hurt her, but he should protect her if she is threatened. When he is strolling along with a girl on the street, he should walk on the outside, nearer the cars. That is symbolic of his responsibility to take care of her.

____ I've taught this principle.

____ I don't agree with this principle.

____ I hope to teach this principle.

____ I agree with this principle,
    but don't think I could teach it.

4. When he is on a date, he should pay for her food and entertainment. Also (and this is simply my opinion), girls should not call boys on the telephone—at least not until a committed relationship has developed. Guys must be the initiators, planning the dates and asking for the girl's company. Teach your son to open doors for girls and to help them with their coats or their chairs in a restaurant. When a guy goes to her house to pick up his date, tell him to get out of the car and knock on the door. Never honk. Teach him to stand, in formal situations, when a woman leaves the room or a table or when she returns. This is a way of showing respect for her. If he treats her like a lady, she will treat him like a man. It's a great plan.

____ I've taught these principles.

____ I don't agree with these principles.

____ I hope to teach these principles.

____ I agree with these principles,
    but don't think I could teach them.

---

5. Remind [your sons] repeatedly and emphatically of the biblical teaching about sexual immorality—and why someone who violates those laws not only hurts himself, but also wounds the girl and cheats the man she will eventually marry. Tell them not to take anything that doesn't belong to them—especially the moral purity of a woman.

___ I've taught this principle.

___ I don't agree with this principle.

___ I hope to teach this principle.

___ I agree with this principle,
but don't think I could teach it.

"Some of the ideas I've suggested sound like 'yesterday.' But they still make sense to me because most of them are biblically based. They also contribute to harmonious relationships between the sexes, which will pay dividends for those who will marry. Dr. Michael Gurian said it best: 'Every time you raise a loving, wise, and responsible man, you have created a better world for women.'"

(ADAPTED FROM THE BOOK *BRINGING UP BOYS* BY DR. JAMES DOBSON [TYNDALE HOUSE])

 Try It: How can you teach boys to respect themselves as males, and to respect and protect females? Here are some ideas.

Preschool:
Self-respect. Sit down with your boy and a family photo album (or some home videos). Look together at pictures of male relatives, pointing out their positive traits. Tell

78

your boy about some of the same traits he's displayed—or how he might grow up to be like some of the men. Example: "There's Uncle Ray. He's always been good at fixing cars. You have some Hot Wheels cars, don't you? Maybe you'll be like Uncle Ray someday."

Respect for the opposite sex. If your boy has a sister, enlist his aid next time she cleans her room. Help him to be careful with her toys and other items, showing respect for her by showing respect for her special possessions. If he has no sister, try practicing holding the door open for girls and ladies next time you go to church or the mall.

Protecting the opposite sex. Play an imagination game involving the boy and Mom or an older sister. Pretend that a semi-darkened room in your home is a "scary cave" with snakes or other hazards on the floor. Give the boy a flashlight and tell him that he's the "brave explorer" who must lead Mom or Sister through the cave. Mom or Sister should follow his lead, expressing plenty of gratitude for his courage.

Elementary:
Self-respect. Each week for a month, stage an awards ceremony for the boy or boys in your household. Give out homemade or purchased medals or certificates commending positive, masculine qualities you've observed. Examples: taking the initiative to right a wrong, showing strength in the face of peer pressure, faithfully providing food for a pet.

Respect for the opposite sex. Many boys in this age group are known for an "I hate girls" attitude. Have your boy choose a girl at school or in the neighborhood and encourage him to make a list of the girl's positive traits. To get him thinking, ask questions like, "Have

79

you ever seen her help someone? Does she smile or tell jokes? Is she polite to the teacher? Does she seem to know much about music or geography or baseball?"

Protecting the opposite sex. Ask your boy, "What could you do if you saw a bully threatening a girl at school?" Brainstorm possibilities, from alerting a teacher to physically intervening. Role-play what the boy could do and say in a such a situation.

Adolescence:
Self-respect. Buy your boy a new men's wallet. Put a copy of your favorite picture of him in it, and tell him why it's your favorite. If possible, put a copy of the same picture in your wallet, too, and let him know that you'll be showing it to others when the opportunity arises.

Respect for the opposite sex. If your teen is dating, loan him a camera next time he goes out. Offer to pay for the date if he gets a bystander to take the following photos during the date: a shot of himself opening a door for the girl; a picture of himself helping the girl with her coat; a photo of himself helping the girl with her chair in a restaurant; a picture of the two of them on the sidewalk, with the boy on the street side.

Protecting the opposite sex. Find an appropriate magazine, newspaper, or Internet article about the problem of battered wives or violence against women. Read it, and invite your teen to read it. Discuss it, asking questions like these: "What do you think about a man who acts this way? What attitude do you suppose he has toward women? How do you think God wants a man to deal with anger? If you knew a girl at school was being abused by her boyfriend, what would you do?"

80

QUESTIONS FROM PARENTS & GRANDPARENTS

PURPOSE: To help participants deal with a variety of parenting challenges by closely and lovingly supervising their boys.

PASSAGES: Proverbs 22:6; Matthew 3:16–17

PREPARATION:
- If possible, watch video 10 in advance. Approximate running time: 33 minutes. If you expect your meeting time to be short, see the Introduction to this guide for ideas on adapting the session plan.

- Make sure each person has a copy of the Participant's Guide; you may want to bring extras for visitors.

- Provide pens or pencils.

- Set up a television and video player in your meeting place.

PREVIEW: In this segment, Dr. Dobson fields questions from the audience. Participants ask advice on a variety of topics related to raising boys.

WELCOME
the group

Have two volunteers come to the front of the room. Call one volunteer "Boy" and the other "Parent." Ask the group: **How close should a parent stay to a boy? I'm going to call out various ages and stages of childhood and adolescence, and you tell "Boy" and "Parent" whether they should get closer together or further apart when "Boy" is at those ages and stages.**

Call out the following:

- **Newborn**
- **Age two**
- **Kindergarten**
- **Age eight**
- **Age thirteen**
- **High school**
- **Age twenty-one**

After each age or stage, give group members a few moments to call out their instructions to your volunteers. Don't worry if the group calls out conflicting directions.

Then ask your volunteers: **Was this confusing? Did you agree with the group's advice?**

Ask the group: **What do you think it means to "stay close" to a boy you're raising?**

Then say: **Staying close to a boy can head off a lot of problems. In today's video, audience members ask Dr. Dobson about a variety of boy-raising challenges. Let's see which ones might be dealt with by staying close.**

WATCH
the video

With the group, watch video segment 10, "Questions from Parents and Grandparents." Encourage participants to take notes in the "Video Journal" section of the Participant's Guide. Pass out pens or pencils as needed.

STEP

WRESTLE
with the principles

Discuss the video, using questions and comments along the following lines.

With which of the questions did you most identify? Why?

Did the questions tend to have anything in common? Did the answers?

In his book *Bringing Up Boys*, Dr. Dobson writes that "staying close" is an important way to deal with many boy-raising challenges. What do you suppose he means by "staying close"?

After considering group members' responses, point out that Dr. Dobson recommends staying close to boys in the sense of supervising them vigilantly—and in the sense of maintaining a loving relationship.

Can you think of any biblical examples of these two aspects of staying close?

Have a volunteer read Matthew 3:16–17 from the "Scriptures to Study" section of the Participant's Guide. Discuss the passage, using questions and comments like the following.

What kind of relationship does this passage show between the Father and His Son? (A loving, affirming one.)

What are some other examples from Scripture demonstrating the closeness of Jesus and His Father? (Some possibilities: when Jesus prayed in Gethsemane [Matthew 26:36], or when He was a boy in the Temple, speaking to the leaders about His Father [Luke 2].)

Have a volunteer read Proverbs 22:6 from the Participant's Guide; discuss the passage, using questions and comments like the following.

Do you think "training up" a boy usually requires closer supervision than "training up" a girl? Why or why not?

Can you "train up" a child without staying close emotionally? Why or why not?

Read the following quote from the book *Bringing Up Boys*: "**It still makes sense to prohibit harmful or immoral behavior, but those prohibitions must be supplemented by an emotional closeness that makes children want to do what is right. They must know that you love them unconditionally and that everything you require of them is for their own good....'Laying down the law' without this emotional linkage is likely to fail....The tricky part is to establish those friendships while maintaining parental authority and respect. It can be done. It must be done.**"

Ask: **How can you do that tricky part, offering both rules and relationship? Let's try an exercise that might help.**

Point out the "Apply It" section of the Participant's Guide for people to work on either individually or in groups. Then allow volunteers to share results. As needed, note that fun times together don't have to include overt lessons—and not every bit of guidance has to be delivered during recreation. The point of the exercise is that supervision and emotional closeness can be part of the same relationship.

WRAP UP
the session

In the next session, we'll look at our ultimate priority in raising boys.

Pray for group members, thanking God for the care and concern they show for boys. Ask God to give wisdom in applying these principles this week; if appropriate, include behavioral concerns that were mentioned in discussion.

Call attention to the "Try It" section of the Participant's Guide. Thumbnail versions of these pages are at the end of the session. Encourage people to use the ideas to create emotional closeness while providing guidance for their boys.

Scriptures to Study

"Train a child in the way he should go, and when he is old he will not turn from it."

—PROVERBS 22:6

"As soon as Jesus was baptized, He went up out of the water. At that moment heaven was opened, and He saw the Spirit of God descending like a dove and lighting on Him. And a voice from heaven said, 'This is My Son, whom I love; with Him I am well pleased.'"

—MATTHEW 3:16-17

Apply It:

One way to stay close is to connect through a boy's natural interests. As a first step, think of a boy. Come up with two or three of his favorite activities and write them in the space below.

Now choose one of those activities—one you could spend some time doing together—and write it here.

Next, think of an area in which this boy needs guidance. (Examples: table manners, prayer, being more organized about homework, choosing a career.) Write it below.

83

DR. JAMES DOBSON'S bringing up boys

Now try to think of a parallel between the activity you chose and the guidance the boy needs. For instance, playing basketball takes teamwork; so does getting chores done in a family. Building a baking-soda-and-vinegar volcano requires doing things in the right order; so does getting homework finished. How could you point out that parallel in your own words, without being preachy or negative? Write what you might say.

Try It:

Staying close takes persistence and creativity. Consider some of the following ideas for providing the loving guidance your boy needs.

Preschool:
To teach good behavior, make a "Behavior Calendar." Choose a goal you'd like to see the boy reach. (Examples: to tell the truth about whether he brushed his teeth before bed; to take one more bath per week; to stop pulling the cat's tail.) Make a calendar showing positive and negative repercussions that will occur when the boy achieves or fails to achieve the goal that day or week. For instance, if the goal is "no lying," a daily reward could be an extra story read at bedtime; a penalty might be a "time out."

In addition to daily steps, you may want to offer a bigger prize (a certificate, small trophy, or toy) at the end of the week or month.

84

Elementary:
Instead of asking the generic, "What happened at school today?" and getting a vague response, ask questions like these:

1. If I could have listened to your thoughts during recess today, what would I have heard?

2. Who had the best lunch at your table? Who had the worst?

3. What animal did your teacher most resemble today? Why? What animal were you most like?

4. If you'd been the principal of your school today, what would have been different?

5. What do you deserve a reward for doing at school today?

Adolescence:
Does your teen's social whirl make it tough to stay close?

1. If he doesn't have a cell phone, consider getting or loaning him one when he goes out. It can be a good way for him to let you know where he is, what he's doing, and when something unexpected comes up.

2. Talk in *advance* about what he'll do if alcohol or other drugs appear at an event he's attending. Explain that if he calls, you'll come and get him.

3. Sit down at the beginning of each month and mark your commitments on a calendar. Work out schedule conflicts before they happen.

85

session **11**

THE ULTIMATE PRIORITY

PURPOSE: To help group members understand the importance of cultivating their boys' relationships with God, and to help them plan ways to do so.

PASSAGES: Deuteronomy 6:6–9; Proverbs 3:1–6

PREPARATION:
- If possible, watch video 11, "The Ultimate Priority," in advance. Approximate running time: 43 minutes. If you expect your meeting time to be short, see the Introduction to this guide for ideas on adapting the session plan.

- Make sure each person has a copy of the Participant's Guide; you may want to bring extras for visitors.

- Provide pens or pencils.

- Set up a television and video player in your meeting place.

PREVIEW: Here's a summary of the principles in video 11:

There's a tug-of-war going on for the hearts and minds of children today. Some want to use our children to further their own agendas and manipulate the future of our society. Protecting children is up to parents, who must be willing to pay the price in sacrificing time and energy.

To ensure that children are given the tools they need for adulthood, parents need to balance love and authority. Kids must know that parents are in charge—and that parents love them more than anything else. Bridges must be built between kids and parents early in life, before adolescence strains those ties.

Parents must also get their priorities in order. The ultimate priority is to lead your child to Jesus Christ. The window of opportunity for this to happen tends to be brief, early in a child's life.

By acting on this ultimate priority, parents can help their boys' lives have significance and meaning—and know they did all they could to raise their boys right.

STEP
1

WELCOME
the group

Ask: **What happens if your boys don't get enough of the following?**

- **Food**
- **Water**
- **Physical exercise**
- **Vocational training**
- **Clothing**
- **Spiritual guidance**

Then ask: **If that were a priority list, where would you put "spiritual guidance"? Why?**

Now here's a question to think about, not answer aloud: Are you satisfied with the spiritual training your boys are getting?

After giving people a few moments to consider that, explain:
In today's video, Dr. James Dobson talks about the ultimate priority in raising boys.

WATCH
the video

With the group, watch video segment 11. Encourage participants to take notes in the "Video Journal" section of the Participant's Guide. Pass out pens or pencils as needed.

WRESTLE
with the principles

Discuss the video, using questions and comments along the following lines.

Did this video leave you feeling guilty, inspired, or something else? Why?

Would you agree that leading by example is the best way for Christian parents to teach children about spiritual matters? Why? What are some other ways?

Read the following quote from Dr. Dobson's book *Bringing Up Boys*, **"I believe the greatest sense of fulfillment as you prepare to close the final chapter [of life] will be in knowing that you lived by a consistent standard of holiness before God and that you invested yourself unselfishly in the lives of your family members and friends....Why not determine to live according to that value system now, while you still have the opportunity to influence the impressionable kids who look up to you? This may be the most important question you as a mother or father will ever have to face!"**

Ask: **How have you faced this question so far? Do you feel the need for change in this area? Why or why not?**

Have the group turn to the "Scriptures to Study" section of the Participant's Guide. Read, or have a volunteer read, Deuteronomy 6:6–9. Then ask questions like the following.

According to verse 6, who needs to learn God's commands? (All of us. God's truths are to be on our own hearts—preferably before we try to pass them on.)

What advice does this passage give on how to teach God's commands to children? (Talk about them during everyday activities; put them in prominent places around the house, even on yourself.)

What would be the best places in your home to put Bible verses if you wanted your boys to see them often?

Ask a volunteer to read Proverbs 3:1–6. Then ask questions like these:

According to Solomon, what will following his instruction give his son? (Longer life, prosperity, favor, and a good reputation with God and people.)

After listing these benefits, what is the first instruction Solomon gives? (Trust in the Lord.)

Do the boys you care for understand the importance and benefits of trusting in the Lord? How do you know? If group members would prefer not to share this personal information, just let them think about it.

Have people turn to the "Apply It" section of the Participant's Guide to help them gauge where their boys are spiritually. Thumbnail versions of these pages are at the end of the session. Allow group members to work on this individually. Those who aren't parents of sons should complete the activity with another boy—a relative or neighbor, perhaps—in mind.

Then let volunteers share results. If group members are reluctant to do so, due to the personal nature of the information, don't press. Simply encourage people to use their answers as indicators of areas they need to work on.

WRAP UP
the session

If time allows, form pairs or teams who pray for each other and for their boys—especially for progress in their boys' relationship with God. If your church offers special programs for boys, encourage parents to consider them.

Call attention to the "Try It" section of the Participant's Guide. Thumbnail versions of these pages are at the end of the session. Explain: **Spiritual training can be fun! Here are some activities you can try this week—and a place you can go for more resources.**

"My son, do not forget my teaching,
but keep my commands in your heart,
for they will prolong your life many years
and bring you prosperity.
Let love and faithfulness never leave you;
bind them around your neck,
write them on the tablet of your heart.
Then you will win favor and a good name
in the sight of God and man.
Trust in the LORD with all your heart
and lean not on your own understanding;
in all your ways acknowledge Him,
and He will make your paths straight."

—PROVERBS 3:1–6

 Apply It: Underline the statements you think your son could make at this point in his life. Draw a box around those you think he couldn't truthfully make now, but that you'd like him to be able to be able to make someday.

"I pray on my own about things that matter to me."
"Church is boring."
"I have a personal relationship with Jesus."
"God made the world."
"Christians are hypocrites."
"I read the Bible on my own regularly."
"Jesus loves me."
"I do things to help people who have less than I do."
"I want to follow Jesus."
"I don't get anything out of Sunday school."
"I like going to church."

"I understand most of what I read in the Bible."
"Religion isn't a 'guy thing.'"
"My faith makes a difference in my decisions."

 Try It: Have some family fun—and teach a spiritual principle at the same time. Here are heritage-building ideas adapted from *The Focus on the Family Parents' Guide to the Spiritual Growth of Children* (Tyndale House).

Preschool:
• Make tunnels and tents throughout the house with blankets, card tables, chairs, boxes, and whatever you can find. These are especially great during thunderstorms when you're armed with a flashlight and a big bowl of popcorn to eat. Read Psalm 91 and talk about how God covers us with His love.

• Throw a birthday party for a pet and invite all the neighbor kids. For a dog party, serve children "dog kibble" (Cocoa Puffs); for a cat, serve goldfish crackers; for a bird, serve sunflower seeds. Show how all God's creation is special and worth celebrating.

Elementary:
• Walk on the ceiling with mirrors. For this, you take a hand mirror and hold it about waist height. Look down into it and you will see the ceiling. Begin to walk through the house. Step over any obstacle you see in the mirror. This works best in homes with lots of doorways and ceiling beams. Walking down stairs is a real challenge! Your family can learn that basing your life on man's ideas is much like walking "on the ceiling," while walking in the truth is like seeing life as it really is.

• Make hats out of paper plates and wild and silly objects: toys, dry food, crafts—the more outrageous the better. Everyone must wear his or her hat to dinner and tell a story about the hat. Go to McDonald's or out for ice cream wearing the hats. Pretend to be very serious while people stare at you. Remind your family that everyone is to be prepared to share about the hope that is within them. Their relationship with Jesus makes them "different," and sometimes people might wonder about it.

Adolescence:
• Have a cooperation dinner—everyone must feed the person to his or her left. As Christians, we are to encourage and help one another.

• Make a video called "Arms." This takes two performers. One person stands in front of a table with items on it, like a phone, a bowl of applesauce or cereal, and a pen and piece of paper. This person clasps his hands behind his back. A second person hides behind him and puts his arms through the sleeves of the person in front of him. Now have the standing person speak and tell the story, or say things that involve the items on the table. The "arms" must pick up the phone and hold it to the person's ear, feed him, make hand motions as if he is the person speaking, and so on. Use this to illustrate the idea of not letting ourselves be manipulated by peer pressure into doing things we wouldn't do on our own.

Note: For more ideas on how to teach your children spiritual values, visit the Heritage Builders Web site at www.heritagebuilders.com.

session

12

TAKING ACTION

PURPOSE: To help group members review key principles from this course, and to plan how they'll apply selected principles to raising the boys in their care.

PASSAGES: 1 Chronicles 16:11; Proverbs 15:22; 16:3; Philippians 4:13; James 2:17

PREPARATION:

- Since this is a review session, there is no corresponding video segment to watch. Instead, the group will concentrate on turning the principles of the earlier videos into action.

- Make sure each person has a copy of the Participant's Guide; you may want to bring extras for visitors.

- Provide pens or pencils.

WELCOME
the group

Have people turn to the "Quotes and Questions" portion of the Participant's Guide. Read aloud the following quote from Dr. James Dobson's book *Bringing Up Boys* (Tyndale House):

"Prayer is the key to everything. I'm reminded of a story told by a rookie player for the Chicago Bulls in the National Basketball Association. One night, the incomparable Michael Jordan scored sixty-eight points, and the rookie was sent in for the last couple of minutes of the game. When the young man was interviewed by a reporter afterwards, he said, 'Yeah, it was a great night. Michael Jordan and I scored sixty-eight points.' That's the way I feel about parenting and prayer. We do all we can to score a few points, but the greater contribution is made by the creator of children."

Ask: **Of all the principles discussed in this course, which one do you think you'll need the most supernatural help to apply? Why?**

After listening to replies, move to the prayer-writing activity that follows in the Participant's Guide. If people have completed this before the meeting, let volunteers read what they did; if not, give them a couple of minutes to do the exercise now. Let participants share results if they're comfortable doing so.

Then say: **This video series has given us a lot to think about. But we don't want to stop there. We need to act on the principles Dr. Dobson has presented. We can't do that without God's help—and we can't do it without specific planning. That's what we want to concentrate on in this session.**

WATCH
the video

Ask: **If you had to choose seven of the most important principles from this video series, what would they be?**

Answers will vary, naturally. Affirm as many as you can. Then say: **No doubt there were more than seven ideas worth** remembering in this course. Here are seven we can zero in on during our discussion today:

1. Don't try to eliminate a boy's naturally aggressive and excitable behavior; celebrate, shape, and civilize it.

2. To prevent the "Wounded Spirit" syndrome in a boy, deal decisively with bullies, reduce exposure to violence, and watch for signs of depression.

3. Stay close to your boy, both emotionally and as a vigilant guide; convey rules in the context of a loving relationship.

4. To help a boy develop a healthy gender identity, make sure he receives appropriate affection, attention, and approval from his father (or, in the father's absence, a trustworthy male role model).

5. Spend both quantity and quality time with your boy, even if it means changing your lifestyle to make that time available.

6. Counteract the effects of male-bashing in our culture by affirming a boy's masculinity and his value as a person.

7. Make your boy's relationship with God the first priority as you raise him.

Now, how can we keep from being overwhelmed by all those instructions?

Consider group members' answers if any are offered. Then have them turn to the "Scriptures to Study" section of the Participant's Guide. Ask a volunteer to read Philippians 4:13. Then ask:

Has the Lord ever given you strength to face a parenting challenge? If so, what happened? If possible, be ready with an example of your own to "prime the pump."

Ask someone to read 1 Chronicles 16:11. Then discuss along the following lines.

How do we "look to the Lord" and "seek His face" when we're bringing up boys? (By asking Him for wisdom; by throwing ourselves on His mercy; by looking for answers in the Bible, etc.)

Read Proverbs 15:22. Then ask: **Who have been your advisers when it comes to raising boys? How have they helped?**

As you plan ways to apply what you've learned in this course, how could the rest of us assist you? (Others can share what they've learned through experience; I can test my ideas on them, etc.)

Have someone read Proverbs 16:3. Ask: **How could you "commit to the Lord" your plans for bringing up boys?** (Recognize that I can't do it under my own power; relax and trust Him to help me; seek His input on my plans in the first place, etc.)

Let a volunteer read James 2:17. Then discuss: **What do you suppose James might think of someone who says, "Sure, there were some good ideas in that video series," but doesn't act on any of them?** (He might think the person doesn't really believe in the principles of *Bringing Up Boys*, or that the person doesn't realize that agreement without action is useless.)

So, what actions will you take as a result of this course?

After listening to responses, explain that you want to help people take a first step toward turning ideas into action. Call attention to the "Apply It" section of the Participant's Guide. Have people work on this individually or in groups. To help group members focus on the concerns that most need their attention, encourage them to check no more than five of the items on the list.

After several minutes, regather the whole group and let volunteers share results. Avoid pressing for responses, however, since people may not want to reveal problems they face with their boys.

STEP
3

WRAP UP
up the session

Have everyone turn to the "Try It" section of the Participant's Guide. Thumbnail versions of these pages are at the end of the session. This exercise helps group members plan specific ways and times to follow through on the concerns they expressed in the "Apply It" questionnaire.

If time permits, let participants work on this "Try It" activity for several minutes. Allow them to choose whether to work alone or in teams. If time is short, encourage group members to complete the exercise at home.

To close, form small groups. Participants can choose to tell each other about their action plans if they wish. Group members should then pray for each other, asking God to provide the wisdom and strength needed for each person's plans to succeed.

As you wrap up this series, invite group members to stay in touch with each other and with you as they face the challenge of raising boys. You may want to plan a reunion in a few months to find out how things are going—and to offer added encouragement.

Apply It: **Principle 1: Don't try to eliminate a boy's naturally aggressive and excitable behavior; celebrate and shape and civilize it.**

___ I need to lighten up about "typical boy" activity that's been irritating me.

___ My boy needs more civilizing.

___ I need to let my boy know that I love him the way he is.

Principle 2: To prevent the "Wounded Spirits" syndrome in a boy, deal decisively with bullies, reduce exposure to violence, and watch for signs of depression.

___ My boy faces bullying, and I need to resolve it.

___ My boy sees or hears too much violent entertainment, and I need to intervene.

___ I'm concerned that my boy may be depressed.

Principle 3: Stay close to your boy, both emotionally and as a vigilant guide; convey rules in the context of a loving relationship.

___ I need to be clearer about what the rules are in our home.

___ I do okay as a rule-giver, but I'm afraid the relationship isn't what it should be.

___ I fear I'm losing track of my boy and what he's doing.

96

Principle 4: To help a boy develop a healthy gender identity, make sure he receives appropriate affection, attention, and approval from his father (or, in the father's absence, a trustworthy male role model).

___ I have a hard time showing my son affection.

___ My boy hears more criticism than approval from me.

___ I need to find a good male role model for my boy.

Principle 5: Spend both quantity and quality time with your boy, even if it means changing your lifestyle to make that time available.

___ I'm not spending enough time with my boy.

___ We spend time together, but I don't think he gets much out of it.

___ I'm so busy that my life is out of control.

Principle 6: Counteract the effects of male-bashing in our culture by affirming a boy's masculinity and his value as a person.

___ I need to talk with my boy about antimale messages he sees on TV or in the movies.

___ My boy's education is suffering because of antimale bias in the school system.

___ My boy needs to learn more respect for himself and for the opposite sex.

97

Principle 7: Make your boy's relationship with God the first priority as you raise him.

___ I need to take better advantage of "teachable moments" with my boy.

___ I fear negative experiences at church or at home may be decreasing my boy's interest in God.

___ I need to be more intentional about encouraging my boy to accept Jesus as Savior.

Try It: **1. Dealing with boyishness**

___ I need to lighten up about "typical boy" activity that's been irritating me.

Action: Next time this boy is rambunctious (without being disobedient), I'll respond by…

___ My boy needs more civilizing.

Action: This week I will begin to teach this boy that "good manners" include…

___ I need to let my boy know that I love him the way he is.

Action: During the next 24 hours, I will tell this boy…

98

2. Preventing "Wounded Spirit" syndrome

___ My boy faces bullying, and I need to resolve it.

Action: This week I will speak to the bully's parents or school authorities, and tell them…

___ My boy sees or hears too much violent entertainment, and I need to intervene.

Action: This week I'll tell this boy that he may no longer watch (or listen to)…

___ I'm concerned that my boy may be depressed.

Action: During the next 24 hours, I will talk to the boy about his feelings; if he seems truly depressed, I will make an appointment for the two of us to see…

3. Staying close

___ I need to be clearer about what the rules are in our home.

Action: This week I'll call a family meeting to discuss…

___ I do okay as a rule-giver, but I'm afraid the relationship isn't what it should be.

99

Action: This week I'll ask my spouse or a friend for an honest assessment of whether my behavior toward this boy might be too...

____ I fear I'm losing track of my boy and what he's doing.

Action: During the next 24 hours I'll sit down with the boy and find out...

4. Gender identity

____ I have a hard time showing my son affection.

Action: During the next 24 hours I will give the boy an around-the-shoulder hug whenever...

____ My boy hears more criticism than approval from me.

Action: During the next 24 hours I will compliment him at least three times about...

____ I need to find a good male role model for my boy.

Action: This week I will talk with a pastor or another man I trust to get suggestions on...

5. Spending time

____ I'm not spending enough time with my boy.

Action: I will set aside the following block of time on the following day this week...

____ We spend time together, but I don't think he gets much out of it.

Action: This week I'll ask the boy to make a list of the top ten things he'd like the two of us to do together, and then I'll...

____ I'm so busy that my life is out of control.

Action: This week I'll ask my spouse or a friend to help me slow down by cutting out...

6. Countering antimale bias

____ I need to talk with my boy about antimale messages he sees on TV or in the movies.

Action: This week we'll watch and discuss...

____ My boy's education is suffering because of antimale bias in the school system.

Action: This week I'll make an appointment to talk with the following teacher or administrator...

____ My boy needs to learn more respect for himself and for the opposite sex.

Action: This week I'll model a respectful relationship with my spouse or, if I'm single, with an opposite-sex friend by...

7. Introducing a boy to God

____ I need to take better advantage of "teachable moments" with my boy.

Action: During the next 24 hours, I will look for at least two times when the boy seems open to talking about...

____ I fear negative experiences at church or at home may be decreasing my boy's interest in God.

Action: This week I'll ask the boy to tell me honestly how he feels about...

____ I need to be more intentional about encouraging my boy to accept Jesus as Savior.

Action: This week I'll call the boy's Sunday school teacher, youth leader, or pastor, and ask how I could...

FOCUS ON THE FAMILY®

Welcome to the Family!

Whether you received this book as a gift, borrowed it from a friend, or purchased it yourself, we're glad you read it! It's just one of the many helpful, insightful, and encouraging resources produced by Focus on the Family.

In fact, that's what Focus on the Family is all about—providing inspiration, information, and biblically based advice to people in all stages of life.

It began in 1977 with the vision of one man, Dr. James Dobson, a licensed psychologist and author of 16 best-selling books on marriage, parenting, and family. Alarmed by the societal, political, and economic pressures that were threatening the existence of the American family, Dr. Dobson founded Focus on the Family with one employee—an assistant—and a once-a-week radio broadcast, aired on only 36 stations.

Now an international organization, Focus on the Family is dedicated to preserving Judeo-Christian values and strengthening the family through more than 70 different ministries, including eight separate daily radio broadcasts; television public service announcements; 13 publications; and a steady series of books and award-winning films and videos for people of all ages and interests.

Recognizing the needs of, as well as the sacrifices and important contribution made by, such diverse groups as educators, physicians, attorneys, crisis pregnancy center staff, and single parents, Focus on the Family offers specific outreaches to uphold and minister to these individuals, too. And it's all done for one purpose, and one purpose only: to encourage and strengthen individuals and families through the life-changing message of Jesus Christ.

• • •

For more information about the ministry, or if we can be of help to your family, simply write to Focus on the Family, Colorado Springs, CO 80995 or call 1-800-A-FAMILY (1-800-232-6459). Friends in Canada may write Focus on the Family, P.O. Box 9800, Stn. Terminal, Vancouver, B.C. V6B 4G3. or call 1-800-661-9800. Visit our Web site—www.family.org—to learn more about Focus on the Family or to find out if there is an associate office in your country.

We'd love to hear from you!

Notes:

Notes:

_____

_____

_____

_____

_____

_____

_____

_____

_____

_____

_____

_____

_____

_____

_____

_____

_____

_____